KERRY NELSON SELMAN

CRYSTAL RESONANCE

Combining Gemstones, Essential Oils &
Flower Essences for Enhanced Well-Being

Llewellyn Publications
Woodbury, Minnesota

FIRST EDITION
First Printing, 2015

Book design by Bob Gaul
Chakra and aura illustrations: Mary Ann Zapalac
Cover design by Kevin R. Brown
Cover art: iStockphoto.com/6571433/©Martinan
 iStockphoto.com/8023292/©aist1974
 iStockphoto.com/16155746/©Nadanka
 iStockphoto.com/16894253/©STILLFX
 Shutterstock.com/73491988/©afitz
 Shutterstock.com/166413185/©Wlad74
 Shutterstock.com/131088674/©Wlad74
 Shutterstock.com/146395481/©MAC1
Editing by Ed Day
Interior crystal and color insert photography: Llewellyn art department,
 except for Selenite and Tiger Iron © Andy Frame Photography
Additional image: iStockphoto.com/16894253/©STILLFX

Llewellyn Publications is a registered trademark of Llewellyn Worldwide Ltd.

Library of Congress Cataloging-in-Publication Data (Pending)
978-0-7387-4394-3

Llewellyn Publications
A Division of Llewellyn Worldwide Ltd.
2143 Wooddale Drive
Woodbury, MN 55125-2989
www.llewellyn.com

Printed in the United States of America

Amethyst

Aquamarine

Aventurine, Green

Citrine

Carnelian

Fluorite

Jasper, Red

Moonstone

Quartz, Clear

Quartz, Rose

Selenite

Tiger Iron

Tourmaline, Black

CRYSTAL
RESONANCE

© Jill Dolby, LoJo Photography, Canbera Australia

To Write the Author

If you wish to contact the author or would like more information about this book, please write to the author in care of Llewellyn Worldwide, and we will forward your request. Both the author and the publisher appreciate hearing from you and learning of your enjoyment of this book and how it has helped you. Llewellyn Worldwide cannot guarantee that every letter written to the author can be answered, but all will be forwarded. Please write to:

Kerry Nelson Selman
℅ Llewellyn Worldwide
2143 Wooddale Drive
Woodbury, MN 55125-2989

Please enclose a self-addressed stamped envelope for reply,
or $1.00 to cover costs. If outside the USA, enclose
an international postal reply coupon.

Many of Llewellyn's authors have websites with additional information and resources. For more information, please visit www.llewellyn.com.

Contents

Foreword

Reading *Crystal Resonance*, I loved its simplicity, warmth, rawness, and honesty.

I am a big fan of any resource that provides not only information but also the opportunity for others to learn new skills. I like the "see, look, feel, and do" method of learning and I especially like anything that can be easily implemented and directly applied. Anyone with an interest in crystals, aromatherapy, flower essences, healing, and the body/mind connection will enjoy this book. It has plenty of juicy information waiting to be savored and it's an easy read.

Kerry's love and devotion of the Earth, herbs, and plants shine vividly through her pen. How could they not? Her mother grew herbs and enjoyed psychic connection; her grandmother both grew and gathered herbs and made her own herbal blends and creams; her great-grandmother brought her connection to the Elementals with her from Ireland; and her great-grandfather was a nurseryman and orchardist, to name but some. It is "in the blood." She also has a fascination with Celtic and Druid History.

Kerry is widely read and has learned much from adversity and the School of Hard Knocks. Her desire to change, to adapt, and to grow, and learn from her mistakes and experiences has brought her to the door of a wonderful place.

Through guidance and a bit of push and shove from teachers over the years, Kerry has become a serious seeker and, through her study, has found a way to link valuable resources in a way that complements and synthesizes much of what she has learned. In the past decade, she has studied and completed many courses which I believe have fast-tracked her self-development, use of her skills, and ability to willingly share her knowledge. She has learned the difference between caring about, and caring for, and allowing.

I felt a yearning for nourishment and a deep inner feeling for nurturing as I was reading *Crystal Resonance*. I found myself wanting to get started, wanting to try out some of Kerry's combinations. It was as if the book was reaching out and telling me it was time to be at home—time to allow and time to yield; home being the internal inner mystery, far beyond the external, material me.

Be true to thine own self, there is a buried treasure waiting to be found within. It is time to be. The Alchemist is calling us home. And, at last, she has arrived.

Margot Deepā Slater (now known as Margotdeepā Slater-Oliphant)
Creator of Newlife Reiki Seichim
Merimbula NSW
Australia

Thanks and Appreciation

Heartfelt gratitude to all those family members, friends, teachers, and mentors who have contributed to my growth and, from time to time, walked with me along my spiritual and experiential path. I am grateful to all those who have taken time to share their talents, passions, and teachings, which have in turn informed, inspired, and facilitated my unfolding life experience. It has been a life rich in texture and experience and I would not have missed any of it!

The scenic route has been explored when I could have opted for the more direct one; I have been a traveler when I could have fast-tracked; I have hung on to mental and emotional pain when I did not know I could just let it go; I have reveled in the highs, savoring every last drop; but the rich tapestry I have woven is uniquely mine and has served me well because it has brought me here. Had I not been there, I could not be here; I love where I am, and bubble with expectancy about where I am heading.

Divine guidance, love, and inspiration constantly and unconditionally nourish, nurture, support, and sustain me; Spirit is ever present, flowing to me, through me, and from me, and I register my unlimited appreciation and gratitude for the awareness that I now have of it. The gifts are limitless, the freedom breathtaking, and the love and light strong, a beacon to bring me back to where I choose to be. I choose to live in the wonder of life: it is there that I thrive; it is from there that I can facilitate others being however they choose to be … and all that they choose to be. We all shine so brightly.

I am also profoundly grateful for the unwavering, unlimited and unconditional love, patience, and support of my husband, Gary, who always encourages me to fly and never doubts that we can. I have been blessed to share this Life experience with him.

Kerry Nelson Selman

Introduction

We can never be sure where those first few moments of any new awareness will take us. My awareness of the synergistically combined gifts from Mother Earth has brought me home to a place of wonder, to that place where I feel a connection to Spirit. It is where I feel I belong and where I now choose to be.

The synergistically combined gifts from the Earth and Beyond help us thrive as we embrace self-responsibility, self-determination, self-respect, and self-worth. We feel empowered to be all that we choose to be, to feel grounded and supported, and to have an appreciation of the unlimited gifts available to us. We are meant to thrive; of that there is no doubt.

I now wish to share this new way for us to connect to All That Is, and enjoy enhanced wellness and well-being based purely on resonance frequency as perceived through a loving heart and Reiki hands. The synergistic combinations that I share have served me well in my practice as a facilitator of wellness and well-being for others and as part of my own daily practice. This information is intended to add to the wealth of knowledge we have so far amassed; it is not intended to replace or contradict methods that may be working for many.

Using the rocks from the earth and precious oils and essences from the plants can help us tap into the innate strength of Gaia, in order to align and attune with Mother Earth. It is no accident that each of us has a body made up of the very same elements as the earth. The awareness that our physical bodies are "of the earth," so to speak, can often spark curiosity to explore and appreciate the gifts that support and surround us.

When we match the resonance of crystal stones and essences with the resonance of specific essential oils and flower essences, and then allow them to dance with the vibrations of Higher Self, Archangels, and Spirit, then indeed we are allowing ourselves to open to and receive the abundant gifts from the Earth and All That Is. I include specific Archangels in these combinations because they represent aspects of Divinity. The practice is simple, and the process is easy and fun: clean and clear crystals with the appropriate essential oil, take the matching crystal and flower essence blend, inhale the essential oil from a tissue or vaporize the oil in a burner, and meditate with your crystal. As you go about your day, carry your anointed crystal enfolded in a handkerchief or a tissue imbued with a few drops of the essential oil, and inhale the crystal-charged essential oil as you wish throughout the day. You may even apply a little matching aromatherapy massage oil to indulge your body and Spirit, and then enjoy the reassuring moments of wonder at the grounded support and enhanced awareness of connection to All That Is as you go about your day. The magic is in the synergy of the combination.

The stories included in the combination descriptions are based on some of my personal moments of struggle, as well as many moments of wonder. We are all such complex creatures, each of us capable of extraordinary creativity— we create great joy but we more often create such unnecessary struggle in our efforts to control and organize everything. Life can and should be simple— but, as I so often acknowledge with clients, simple does not always feel easy.

We so often acknowledge what is not working for us, emphatically decide to embrace positive change, and then seek to manipulate and control exactly how it should occur—thereby creating more struggle and, inevitably, frustration and disappointment. I have been highly skilled at setting unachievable timetables and continually raising the bar of achievement—I have been highly creative and successful at self-sabotage.

However, it is but one of the many creative talents that I now happily own and acknowledge. Each of us can be highly talented in thoughts and actions that do not serve us well, and so I openly share some experiences with you in the hope that moments of awareness and association will likewise be triggered within you—the *ah-ha* moments that might encourage you to explore the synergistic combinations of these gifted tools from the Earth and Spirit that can so powerfully support any steps toward self-responsibility and self-determination; enhance a sense of self-respect, self-value, and self-worth; and ease any decision to change and embrace choices that support, nurture, and sustain us and serve the highest good.

As a holistic practitioner of natural therapies, I am well aware that a vital component of wellness and well-being is the healing and rebalancing that must take place mentally and emotionally. We are gifted so much by Mother Earth, and when specific crystals are matched with the highest resonating essential oils and flower essences, our natural access to Oneness is powerfully facilitated. Healing on every level is enhanced, and a sense of wholeness is restored as the physical, mental, emotional, and spiritual bodies are aligned and attuned. Our bodies are magnificent mechanisms that continually seek homeostasis on every level; homeostasis is our innate natural balance or equilibrium.

In 2013, my appreciation of synergy, curiosity about what is possible, passion for simplicity, and inspiration coalesced to develop these crystal synergistic combinations as a healing and self-enhancing lifestyle practice that restores balance and brings awareness to our inherent wellness and well-being. I have learned that particular crystals, essential oils, and flower essences can be synergistically combined for optimal resonance frequency that enhances connection with specific aspects of Divinity—a synergistic combination offers so much more than the sum of its component parts because each component enhances the other. The wonder of synergy has been long appreciated by those working with herbal medicine and aromatherapy. Indeed, are we not all so much more than our component parts?

The thirteen synergistic combinations in this book encompass the most popular crystals from the practice. (There are simply far too many crystal synergistic combinations to describe each in detail.) For each you will learn about the specific crystal, and the highest resonance pairing of essential oil and flower essences to enhance vibration of all, and how this heightened energy of the whole combination can help you connect with your Higher Self, Spirit, and All That Is. The thirteen crystal combinations were chosen in exactly the same way I choose the crystal synergistic combination each morning for my own daily practice, which I have detailed in the section called "Bringing All the Gifts Together." This practice has served me well, and I trust that it will serve the highest good for each and all of you as you find combinations that resonate with you. When I reviewed the list of combinations, I was delighted to see that it included the most often used combinations, some of the most popular crystals, and some of the combinations that could be considered the most self-empowering.

All crystal stones and essences, plant oils and plant essences, and celestial beings resonate with each other … there are no right or wrong combinations when working with the gifts from the Earth and Beyond. However, there are some gifts that work synergistically to produce a vibration that opens and aligns the chakras to warm the heart and lift us to a place of Oneness that facilitates vibrational wellness and well-being. We are fully supported by the Earth and the Universe. The synergistic crystal combinations in this book are those that consistently offered the highest alignment of resonance … and with which I have therefore worked, and continue to work, with wondrous results.

This book contains but a taste of the bountiful smorgasbord of gifts that support wellness and well-being. The gifts from the Earth and Spirit are limitless. Indeed, it is my intention that these thirteen crystal synergistic combinations and practices might introduce new concepts to those looking to explore working with crystals; expand the knowledge base of those who already use and enjoy crystals, as well as essential oils and flower essences; or enhance the awareness of those who enjoy connection to the realm of Spirit. There is something for all, at every level. If an alternative practice feels right for you at this time, then please honor that and continue as you have been personally guided. If you are curious to explore the synergy of these crystal combinations and feel a sense of excitement and anticipation at the wonders on offer, then you are invited to enjoy.

A full description of crystal therapy, aromatherapy, and flower essence therapy, and the wide-ranging treatment applications, particularly for physical ailments, is beyond the intention and scope of this book. However, many mental, emotional, and spiritual benefits do feature in each description as this is where all healing begins—and is so often the missing link to physical wellness and well-being.

In *Crystal Resonance* I willingly share synergistic combinations and practices that have taken my enjoyment and wonder of crystals and other vibrational tools from the Earth to another level. However, I am well aware that my personal interpretation of connections will sometimes differ from many traditional practices. Nothing in this book is intended to counter or replace those practices that are successfully practiced and embraced by many; I simply offer alternatives that you may wish to explore to extend your current practice.

So please, enjoy those gifts that are available to you and to which you feel drawn, and perhaps among the selection of synergistic combinations offered you may find a little extra something—another layer that facilitates your return to balance and alignment, and enhances and enriches your path to Oneness and vibrational wellness and well-being.

PART ONE

Key Players in Your Crystal Work

Understanding the Energy Body

The great philosophers and avatars across the ages have taught us that everything is in a state of flux, ever-changing. Modern science has confirmed that everything is in a constant state of vibration and is made up of energy. We are energy. Our complex physical bodies are nourished and sustained as energy continually transforms and cycles from thermal, to mechanical, to electrical, to kinetic, and to other forms of energy—vibration, movement, and change are basic to life. Without movement we cannot grow, physically, mentally, emotionally, or spiritually.

Movement and vibration are integral to matter, and to watch the waltz of the atoms is to view the waltz of the solar system, and so the Universe—to see the spinning dance of particles around the atom's nucleus as a perfect indicator of the broader view is to stand in wonder of the perfection of it all. Planet Earth that supports us is in constant change: mountains rise and fall; rivers rise and fall flowing nutrients through to nourish, sustain, and facilitate change; oceans ebb and flow with Divine rhythm, evaporate and return as nourishing rain to continue the cycle; the winds of change blow to facilitate movement, transformation, and life.

Likewise in our bodies, the heart pumps life-giving energy for the lungs to rise and fall to take in air, to be inspired by life force, and for the rivers of blood and lymph to circulate nourishment and cleanse away waste to promote life—even at our most still, we are movement. Protons, neutrons, and electrons waltz within and around the nucleus in a unified dance inside every atom—the particles vibrate, the nano-particles inside the particles vibrate. Vibration of the atoms in every cell, of every tissue, of every organ, of every body system is at the core of our physical bodies. There is perfection, order, harmony, and balance in the dance.

So, too, is there a harmony of vibration between the body physical and the surrounding subtle bodies. The subtle bodies are energetic fields that surround our denser physical body: the Etheric body (also known as Aura or Biomagnetic field), the Emotional (or Astral) body, the Mental body, and the outer Spiritual (or Causal) bodies. The outer spiritual body protects the energy body, like a fine permeable membrane, while connecting us to the greater Universal body. The energy transfer is two-way. There is no separation. Energy constantly flows into, out from, and between the bodies—giving and receiving in equal measure.

The recurring nature of physical ailments treated without healing the outer mental and emotional bodies can serve to remind us that basic issues remain unresolved—what a wonderful indicator the physical body is! When we heal the physical without healing the mental and emotional bodies, that disharmony remains in our energy system and illness recurs or presents in another way to remind us that this issue remains unresolved. By working with the crystal synergistic practices, we aim to finally resolve and heal.

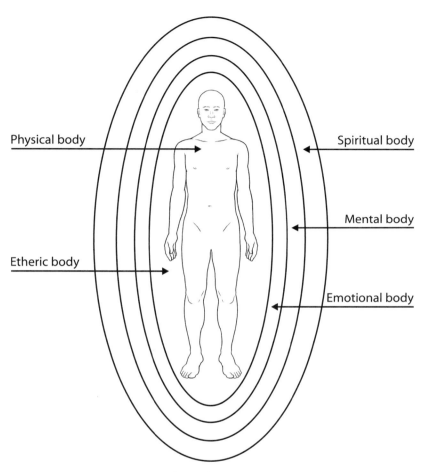

Physical body

Spiritual body

Mental body

Etheric body

Emotional body

The Subtle Bodies

Emotional, mental, and physical healing, together with ongoing wellness and well-being, are always facilitated by cleansing and balancing the subtle bodies. The bodies physical, emotional, mental, and spiritual may be perceived as distinct layers but they are not separate; there is no separation and the harmonizing energy flow of every layer is integral to the whole. Long-held negative beliefs and fixed perspectives and attitudes are now well documented as negatively impacting health.

We live in a world of vibration, separated by only frequency of vibration. The heavy dense energy that is matter, and that which presents as the body physical and medications, vibrates at a different frequency to the subtle matter of essences. Vibrational medicines such as crystal and flower essences, which are embraced in the synergistic combinations, are high-frequency treatments to connect into the high-frequency subtle bodies.

A number of ancient Eastern traditions have given us an appreciation of the chakras, which, without getting into the various philosophies, are energy wheels throughout the body. It is basic to understanding the energy body and energy centers that we regard them as holographic, three-dimensional, surrounding the whole of the body physical; the subtle bodies do not sit flat, adjacent to the body, as they appear on the page. The chakras are no different; they are located on the body physical in figurative drawings, but they actually radiate or spiral their energy out in all directions from their center, each of which is located inside the body, toward the spine. There are seven major chakras, and it is on these main energy centers that we will focus, and that I will now briefly describe.

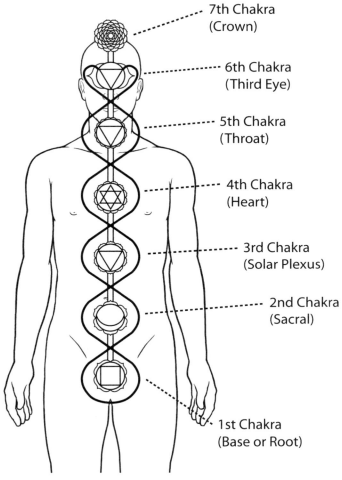

7th Chakra
(Crown)

6th Chakra
(Third Eye)

5th Chakra
(Throat)

4th Chakra
(Heart)

3rd Chakra
(Solar Plexus)

2nd Chakra
(Sacral)

1st Chakra
(Base or Root)

The Seven Chakras

Base or Root (1st) Chakra

The base chakra is located near the base of the spine. It is our foundation, the seat of our vitality, that place from which the impulses of life arise to flow through the body to flower at the crown chakra. It stimulates our basic survival instincts and our basic human potentialities.

Our roots as human beings and our connection to Mother Earth are stored in this chakra. It clarifies our desires and encourages us to stand on our own two feet, knowing our body's requirements and our mind's desires can be met. When our base chakra is healthy, we are grounded and balanced; it supports our ability to provide for ourselves in all areas. Red is the color of the base chakra.

Sacral (2nd) Chakra

The sacral chakra, which means sacred, is located in the sacrum toward the base of the spine—on the front of the body this translates to about 5 centimeters below the navel. It is the energy wheel of creativity and sexuality that circulates nourishing energy throughout the whole body. It is the traditional space of the Zen Knowing Mind, or Hara, and relates to the unconscious mind and its storehouse of instinctive knowing formed from past impressions and previous experiences. When balanced, it allows a warm acceptance of life to flow.

It is connected to the water element and governs our creativity and emotions, relating to our sense of self-worth, self-confidence, and the way we relate to others. The feelings of others are perceived through this chakra; it is one of our centers of extrasensory perception. Orange is the color of the sacral chakra.

Solar Plexus (3rd) Chakra

This is the home of our solar plexus—a position of immense vitality, that place from where we choose to radiate love and support to ourselves and to others in a steady, balanced, and life-enhancing manner. It is our center of personal power, self-will, and achievement—our powerhouse. It is the center of motivation that supports our commitment to life.

A balanced solar plexus chakra finds us able to choose wisely and to achieve the results we intend; we find our own unique gifts, our passions, and fulfillment. We are in balance, able to focus and courageously achieve our goals from our innate powerhouse of reserves. Yellow is the color of the solar plexus chakra.

Heart (4th) Chakra

Located at the heart center, the heart chakra allows us to receive all that the heart can give. An open heart is transformational because it enables us to resolve conflict and raise our awareness, bringing in compassion and empathy. Our emotions are purified in our hearts, allowing more joy and love to enter. This energy center also encompasses our transpersonal heart, opening us to unconditional love, compassion, and understanding. Love does make us strong.

This is at the center of the seven chakras—it is the bridge between the bottom three base chakras and the three higher chakras, that which balances our intellectual instincts and inspiration with our basic physical vitality and instincts of survival. Green (or pink in some traditions) is the color of the heart chakra.

Throat (5th) Chakra

Located in the throat center and throat region of the spinal cord, this is the purification center, the center of communication, and the center of growth— growth seen as another form of expression. This chakra helps ensure we are heard and enhances our ability to confidently and clearly speak our truth.

Communication takes place on many levels: communication with others, and communication within our bodies, between our body, mind, and spirit. Balance in the throat chakra enables us to understand the body's physical, mental, and emotional signals and meet our own needs and honor that which we are with unconditional love and compassion. Blue is the color of the throat chakra.

Third Eye (6th) Chakra

Located in the midbrain behind the eyebrow center, this is our clairvoyant eye, that which sees beyond physical and intellectual knowing and, as such, is the home of our intuition and inspiration, where intellect and Spirit meet, and our center of visualization.

It is the "control center," that place where everything merges into one stream of consciousness; it is integral to the harmonious interplay of body, mind, emotion, and Spirit. Our eyes are regarded as the gateway to the soul. The light from us shines out to others through our eyes; the light of the world shines to us through our eyes. Indigo or purple are the colors of the third eye chakra.

Crown (7th) Chakra

The crown chakra relates to our spirituality and our connection to our Higher Self and the Divine. It is the chakra of higher consciousness. When the crown chakra is balanced, we function with awareness of our connection to Oneness, supported by Divine love and as such, we are able to just *be*, content in the Divine knowledge that there is no need to *do*, just *be*. We find peace in the acceptance of allowing what is, to just be. Meditation is considered key to developing and balancing the crown chakra. Violet, gold, or white are the colors associated with the crown chakra.

....

The following chart indicates the match of some of the thirteen crystals from our synergistic combinations to the chakras, based purely on color.

Chakras	Chakra Colors	Crystal
Base (1st)	Red	Red Jasper
Sacral (2nd)	Orange	Carnelian
Solar Plexus (3rd)	Yellow	Citrine
Heart (4th)	Green or Pink	Green Aventurine, Fluorite, Rose Quartz
Throat (5th)	Blue	Aquamarine, Moonstone
Third Eye (6th)	Purple, Indigo	Amethyst, Fluorite
Crown (7th)	Violet, Gold, or White	Amethyst, Selenite, Moonstone

If you are an energy worker or have an awareness of chakras, you may wish to choose a stone because of its healing color and association with a particular chakra. Energetic healers and color therapists know that every color has a vibrational frequency; the auric field also vibrates with color and colored stones can harmonize the body's energy field and balance the chakras. Archangels, likewise, are seen to vibrate particular halo colors. Matching halo and chakra colors with stone colors are valid and successful crystal healing practices that are embraced by many.

Accepting that we live in a world of vibration, that the body physical is vibrating down to the subatomic particles in each atom of the nucleus heart of each cell, and that likewise the physical body is a vibrational entity surrounded by the vibrational layers of the subtle bodies, protected and connected to all by the external spiritual body may help you appreciate the possibilities on offer from the synergy of the crystal combinations in Part Two.

Everything is vibration, and all vibrational therapies give us tools to help restore harmony and balance to our whole being. Thoughts are energy yet to be manifested, but they exist as vibrations within us and extend out from us. Negative thoughts and entrenched negative beliefs produce disharmony in the subtle bodies, and discord in the vibrational patterns at a cellular level of the physical body, manifesting as disease if left unaddressed. The synergy of the crystal combinations and practices in *Crystal Resonance* offer transformational and life-enhancing support to willingly release and let go of that negative patterning.

The choice remains with each of us to do that which feels right for us, accept self-responsibility, and accept the support offered by the gifts from Mother Earth to powerfully ground us, empower us, and uplift us as we embrace the process and decide to change and let go of those negative thoughts, beliefs, and practices that are limiting us, preventing us from being all that we wish to be.

A description of the energy body that sits well with me comes from those teachings that describe the subtle bodies or aura being comprised of *prana, life force,* or *chi* that flows through the body physical and supports every living being—this encapsulates the sense of innate connection between the energy body of each sentient being and the greater energy body of All That Is.

Bringing All the Gifts Together

Crystal stones from Mother Earth bring many healing and sustaining properties, but the overarching properties common to most are support, protection, and alignment. Working with crystals, we gift ourselves time to just be, time to connect to our place of inner peace and harmony, our Higher Self.

Minerals are as old as Mother Earth, and crystals are highly evolved minerals. Crystals hold many of the characteristics in the organic plant kingdom that followed the planet's evolutionary path, such as self-organization, reproduction via seed crystals, and receiving and transferring information. Crystal essences bring the life-force energy that is as old as time from the inorganic base that supports Mother Earth, therefore crystal essences hold less karmic association than essences from the organic plant kingdom, which holds memory across time. With their non-crystalline structure, plants are more flexible and adaptable in response to memory at both a cellular and subtle level. Blending both crystal and flower essences in this synergistic practice gifts us the healing and realigning properties of both natural gifts from the Earth, with each taking the other to another level.

Plant essential oils, likewise, have many healing properties, but basically these precious oils stimulate or relax our body, mind, and spirit, often concurrently as each subtle body receives that which it requires. The power of deep relaxation and the healing that comes from a sense of relief should never be underestimated. Relaxation stimulates the immune system in the body physical; relaxation brings a sense of well-being to every level of our being.

The subtle healing actions of flower essences are also wide-ranging, but one could say that their actions overwhelmingly correct fear in all of its negative manifestations in the body, mind, and spirit. They are catalysts for change; they support any choice we make to release, rebalance, restore, and reconnect to our innate wellness and well-being.

And so we can begin to appreciate the potential balance that can flow from the perfect marriage between these precious gifts from the earth: crystals protect, strengthen, fortify, and balance our body, mind, and spirit; essential oils encourage balance by stimulating and uplifting, and relaxing and calming, as required; and flower essences act to realign our mind and emotions, and in turn the body, and therefore return us to balance and unity with our Divine life force.

Independently, each modality offers well documented support for our wellness and well-being; brought together and allowed to harmonize, we receive the benefits of the perfect balance of the feminine and masculine energies.

If we then choose to add awareness of connection to our Inner Being or Higher Self, Archangels, or Spirit guides, then miracles happen as we start to live in the wonder of a life that often feels truly magical. Divine life force constantly flows to and through every living thing on this planet and, for me, our Divinity is expressed through our humanity—and we get to choose whether we wish to allow our Divinity to shine in every choice we make, in every moment. It is in the smallest of moments that the biggest choices are made, and it is in these very moments that miracles happen.

The small overview of the component parts of each combination in Part Two is intended to bring an appreciation of their inclusion in the combination and provide an indication of the combination's potential synergy. When I began this exploration my first moment of awareness was how powerfully the identified essential oil enhanced the crystal's actions, and together they were so much more than component parts. My curiosity was ignited, and so began my exploration that led to the crystal synergistic combinations and practices.

Crystals

How Crystals Work

The natural crystalline structure of crystal stones imbue them with inherent physical properties that have long been recognized by modern science and technology: crystal radios were embraced in the early twentieth century; and today, crystals are base components of laser and microprocessing technology.

Striking one end of a quartz crystal point with a hammer in a darkened room will cause a flash at the other end, an electrical spark, demonstrating the crystal's transfer of kinetic energy (motion) at one end into electrical energy (the spark) at the other. This innate property of transforming energy is intrinsic to the powerful healing afforded by crystals.

Crystals respond to the natural electrical vibrations of the cells in the body physical, helping to harmonize, stimulate, or relax as required to restore homeostasis, the body's innate equilibrium to which it constantly seeks to return. However, the most powerful healing potential results from transformation of the electrical charge inherent in entrenched negative thoughts. Please remember that we are imbued with free will, and our choosing to release negative beliefs is paramount for lasting change—we always choose, sometimes unconsciously, but we always choose.

The energy that the crystal absorbs is not necessarily the same energy that it emits. Crystals can absorb, store, focus, amplify, transform, transmute, and transmit energy, and they have the ability to store thoughts and intentions as a magnetic charge in their structure. They can therefore be programmed—

programming is simply storing with intent, such as setting an intention or programming the crystal to always work for our highest good and the highest good of all. In essence, thoughts are vibrations, energy. Our thoughts are often fragmented and scattered; the crystal's inherent orderly energy pattern is constant as it radiates the energy of our intention and enhances manifestation. Crystals can therefore transform our meditation experience because their unique structure resonates with the universal field and higher guidance.

Physical healing can be measured and quantified—we love to quantify in our modern era. Shifts in the mental, emotional, and spiritual bodies cannot always be measured and quantified but they can certainly be experienced, embraced, enjoyed, and celebrated. Their inherent properties enable crystals to shift, rebalance, and revitalize all levels of our being as life-force energy is transmitted and amplified through the entire human energy system.

Choosing Your Crystal

Clear quartz is often known as *the master healer*, and indeed it is one of the most versatile crystals gifted from Mother Earth, but as a practitioner I feel that to believe that there is one all-powerful "healer" would be to deny the abundant possibilities and potentialities gifted by other stones—to use just one crystal is to embrace limitation of the gifts on offer from Mother Earth.

So how do we choose? Crystals offer their own vibration, and if you feel your eyes or hands immediately drawn to a particular stone, or feel warmth or tingling or some positive sensory response when you hold a stone, then I would always advocate that you honor that inspiration and choose accordingly. If you are aware of color therapy, energy healing, and the chakras, you may wish to choose a stone according to its balancing or healing color and association with a particular chakra.

Crystals are basic to my daily synergistic practice, and the synergistic combination that would best serve me is often chosen intuitively according to whichever crystal I'm energetically drawn. This can be as simple as the crystal that draws my eye and holds my attention and how it feels in the hand, but most often I use a crystal pendulum. I choose from my crystals in the early hours of each day, and the speed and clarity of the pendulum as it responds purely to the vibration or energy of my Inner Being, Higher Self, and Spirit is reassuring as my physical body is still adjusting to the new day ahead. Indeed, it is through dowsing with a pendulum that the thirteen crystal combinations were chosen for this book. My intention was that the highest good be served.

Pendulum responses are individual and can differ for each of us, so if you wish to use one but are unfamiliar, please test responses for you before you commence. This is as simple as holding the end bead between your fingers, allowing the pendulum to drop and be still, and mentally asking it to show you "yes" and show you "no" and watch which way it swings; alternatively you can say, "My name is Jack" (when it's actually Sue) and note the response, and then say "My name is Sue" (or whatever your name is) and note the response. The pendulum will swing vertically from you in a straight line (up and down), or across from side to side, or in a circle for each response...whichever way it swings is right for you. The simplicity and reliability of allowing my pendulum to swing to "yes" as my eyes scan the crystals from which I am choosing always serves me well, as does the moment of energetic connection to All That Is when I first rise from bed.

So, crystals can be simply chosen according to color, attraction, the properties and gifts inherent in each, or you may choose intuitively in whatever way works for you.

Cleaning, Clearing, and Activating Your Crystal

Cleaning removes the outer dust and grime: simply immerse the crystal in a dish of water and gently towel dry or allow it to dry. Do not use detergent. Soft crystals should *never* be placed in water and, from the selections within this book, this applies to selenite.

Clearing crystals removes the inner psychic dust and grime, the accumulated vibrations from those who have previously handled them or used them. Clearing can be in saltwater baths or by burying them in salt or in the earth, visualization, Reiki, and the popular and gentle smudging. However, for the synergistic practices in this book, crystals are cleared (and simultaneously cleaned) with the essential oil that offers the highest resonance match. If clearing a number of the same crystal, pop them in filtered water with a drop or two of the essential oil; if clearing an individual stone, or soft selenite, gently rub one drop over the stone. Take a moment to hold the stone(s) in your cupped hands with gratitude for the gifts from Gaia, or Mother Earth, and an intention that the highest good be served. This treatment is equally enhancing and activating for your crystal pendulum if you use one.

Always clear a crystal when you first bring it home, if it feels or looks dull, before programming with a new intention, after doing intense emotional work, or if someone else has worked with it.

Activating allows a crystal to refresh and recharge. Clearing and anointing the stone with the essential oil that has the highest resonance match will also activate and recharge your crystal. Remember, synergy brings so much more than the component parts. Embracing these synergistic practices will keep your crystal beautifully cleared and activated to serve your highest good.

Crystal Essences

The powerful vibrations that are constantly emitted from crystals are easily transferred to water. The prepared essence holds the energetic imprint of the stone, which can be seen in a Kirlian photograph taken immediately after the stone is removed from the water. Crystal essences function between homeopathic remedies and flower essences: homeopathics directly and quickly impact the physical body on a molecular level while integrating the subtle bodies; flower essences influence and balance the subtle bodies which in turn gradually influence the physical. The stone's inherent crystalline structure is integrated into the crystal essence enhancing the life force at a molecular level; the karma-free vibrations inherent in crystals amplify our consciousness, therefore supporting and rebalancing our whole energetic being, and enhancing change.

Making Your Crystal Essence

Toxic and friable stones require specific handling. There are no crystals in these crystal combinations that are toxic (such as raw malachite), however please note the second instructions for soft or crumbly stones, which as previously mentioned, include selenite.

The simplest method to make an essence using non-friable and non-toxic crystals is—

- Clean your crystal in salt and then wipe clean— natural crystals are preferred, but not necessary.

- Place the crystal into pure spring water in a clean glass dish.

- Place the bowl in a sunny position (cover if placed outside to protect from insects and litter) and leave the bowl in its sunny position for a minimum of four hours.

Using the sun to activate the crystal essence results in the transfer of higher frequency energy as the life force is integrated into the water and activated by the rays of the sun.

- Remove the stone, and bottle the water in a fifty milliliter amber dropper bottle/s and preserve each with two teaspoons of brandy.

Toxic or fragile stones (such as selenite) must be prepared using the indirect method to ensure no contact with the water.

- Place your soft selenite inside a glass jar and then place the jar in the water and follow the above instructions.

The usual dosage for crystal essences is four drops under the tongue taken four times daily. In these synergistic practices, you may take your crystal essence in this way, or you may combine your crystal and flower essences into one blend. For the latter, you will use your crystal essence as the base liquid for the required drops of combined flower essences. Details are given with preparing the flower essence blends.

Essential Oils

How Essential Oils Work

Aromatherapy is a powerful practice that uses aroma to relax or stimulate and support a return to harmony and balance in the physical, mental, emotional, and spiritual bodies. Today, science can validate only some of the wonder held in this ancient practice; however, we should never underestimate the power of the mind/body connection, the therapeutic value of aroma, nor the power of deep relaxation.

Essential oils give plants their inherent fragrance; they are the "lifeblood" of the plant, unique and essential to each plant; they are vital to its survival. As we inhale the aroma, tiny molecules are carried directly to the brain and deep into the limbic system in the back brain, our primal brain, which in turn links to the pituitary gland, directly affecting mental, emotional, hormonal, nervous, and immune functions; molecules are also drawn into the lungs from where they are transported into our own life-blood and distributed around the body.

Subtle aromatherapy adds another layer by drawing on the subtle energy of the plant, its unique vibration, to bring healing and rebalancing to the subtle bodies. This practice draws on less tangible properties inherent in these gifts from Mother Earth. There is memory in every form of life and as we experience and add to this memory, the plants hold the memory across time and space to be tapped into and tuned in to by those who are drawn to the practice. Subtle aromatherapy massages the aura, dances with the subtle bodies, brings to the psyche and soul that which is needed, and harmonizes every level to facilitate our personal and spiritual growth.

The synergistic practices combine both forms of aromatherapy. The precious life-force energy in plant essential oils facilitates physical, mental, and emotional wellness and well-being, adding more wonder to each synergistic combination.

Choosing Essential Oils

Please be aware that essential oils are not the same as the tiny oil bottles labeled "fragrant oil," which contain synthetics and lack the inherent chemical constituents and healing properties of pure essential oils. The properties inherent in pure essential oils are core to the process; fragrant oils will not carry the healing gifts from Mother Earth.

The label, smell, and price can guide you. For starters, there is no such oil as strawberry essential oil. Smell the oil—fragrant oils are often very sweet or very strong, or smell synthetic. Essential oils will be labeled 100 percent pure essential oil and will display both the plant's common and botanical names, such as Lavender (*Lavandula angustifolia*).

Price is also an indicator of pure essential oils that have been adulterated with cheaper pure essential oils or synthetics. Extraction is painstaking and the delicacy of the plant material determines the method of extraction, and huge amounts of plant material are required to produce small amounts of essential oil. Therefore, cost varies across the range of pure essential oils, so be skeptical if these tiny precious bottles are all priced the same. Find a supplier you trust.

The essential oils in these synergistic combinations have been chosen as those offering the highest resonance match (which means I have matched them according to their harmonious energies, often using a pendulum as previously described). I lived with the crystal and essential oil combination, even subtly inhaling as I slept with the crystal in my pillow slip. It was a matter of wonder and pure delight to me when I then considered all the particular properties of the essential oil, the perfection of the match, and felt the synergy of the combination in meditation.

There are no rights or wrongs when working with these precious oils, but those that combine synergistically with specific crystals, undoubtedly, lift us to a place of heightened vibration, facilitating wellness and well-being, and clearer connection to Spirit.

Using Essential Oils

Although many who purchase essential oils over the counter may be unaware of contraindications, as a professional practitioner I would feel remiss if I did not mention the following general cautions and contraindications that may apply to the essential oils in these synergistic combinations: do not use essential oils during pregnancy without professional advice; if you have sensitive skin, patch test; cease using immediately if there is any skin irritation; do not massage inflamed, infected, or irritated skin; and do not ingest.

The synergistic practices will use the appropriate essential oil to clear the crystal, anoint the crystal, and inhale the aroma. If you would like to extend the synergistic practice by preparing a massage blend, mix 15 drops of the appropriate essential oil in 25 milliliters of carrier oil such as sweet almond, jojoba, or grapeseed oil. This will give you a 3 percent dilution that is safe for skin. If irritation still occurs, dilute the site with more carrier oil and wipe away with a cloth.

Vaporizing essential oils in an oil burner or diffuser enhances emotional wellness, relaxation, and rejuvenation, as well as being highly useful for many physical complaints. These volatile life-enhancing gifts from the plants bring powerful effects to body, mind, and spirit that often defy rational analysis—we do not need to explain it; we can feel it.

Flower Essences

How Flower Essences Work

Flower essences have been used back through time to heal and improve well-being: from the ancient civilizations of Lemuria, Atlantis, and Egypt, across the African and Asian continents, and in traditional cultures, including that of Indigenous Australians.

The healing power of flower essences was revitalized in the twentieth century by Englishman Dr. Edward Bach and Australian naturopath and healer, Ian White. Both emphasized that true healing depends on emotional and mental alignment, allowing our innate connection to Higher Self, and embracing necessary change.

Flower essences are diluted infusions of flowers in water; they enhance awareness and facilitate transformation of limiting beliefs into health-affirming and life-enhancing ones, thus restoring balance to the whole system. They are a form of vibrational healing. Indeed, Gurudas, in *Flower Essences and Vibrational Healing*, asserts that of the three principal vibrational remedies—homeopathics, crystal essences, and flower essences—flowers are the most effective in treating the subtle bodies, opening the meridians, and thus facilitating physical healing. As previously described, crystal essences offer different energy with similar potency and action. We will bring these two essences together in our practice.

Vibrational medicine recognizes that complete healing always comes from within; the body is a self-healing mechanism; if we choose to facilitate that healing by using vibrational gifts from the Earth, then wellness and well-being will radiate through us and from us.

Bach Flower and Australian Bush Flower Essences

The two inspired remedies from Dr. Bach and Ian White are the remedies I use personally and prescribe professionally. However, the specific blending of the two came with the unfolding of this synergistic practice. It was always my intention that these synergistic combinations not only facilitate powerful healing sessions, but also provide the basis for life-enhancing and life-sustaining practices; these flower essences are readily available and can be purchased over the counter, online, or created in the home.

Bach believed that true healing depended upon: awareness of our Divinity within, and the power of that awareness; acceptance that disease is caused by disharmony between soul and personality; willingness to discover the underlying fault causing the disharmony; and releasing the fault by allowing and developing its opposite virtue.

White further developed flower essences using plants from Australia—a land which metaphysically resonates with the wisdom of the ancients. Australian Bush Flower Essences are catalysts to awaken life force and spiritual consciousness to release limiting beliefs, see our potential, and enhance clarity, creativity, strength, intuition, self-esteem, and spirituality.

The prophylactic action of flower essences should not be underestimated; prevention is far more efficient than cure. We are emotional beings and our emotions are wonderful in-the-moment indicators of that which is out of sync—if we let how we feel guide us, great healing is facilitated and ongoing wellness and well-being assured. Emotions affect our health; emotions can indicate that physical imbalance may follow; flower essences balance our emotions. The subtle bodies direct us through our feelings. Restoring balance to the subtle bodies by addressing issues as they arise prevents the imbalance proceeding to illness.

Devotees will already be familiar with the powerful and subtle healing facilitated by flower essences. Here we have the opportunity to expand, explore, and enjoy the higher frequency vibration offered by the blending of the Bach and Australian Bush Flower Essences and their marriage with the gifts from the Earth and Beyond.

Making Your Own Flower Essences

If you grow the particular flower varieties in the synergistic combinations and wish to prepare your own flower essences, I recommend the simple sun method—using the sun as we did with the crystal essences—to integrate and activate the blend:

- Pick flowers on a warm sunny day.

- Fill a clean glass dish with pure spring water.

- Place the flowers in the spring water, covering the surface.

- Place the bowl in a sunny position (cover to protect, if outside) and leave for a minimum of four hours.

The water becomes impregnated with the flowers' vibrational energy, which the sun integrates with the water and activates the life-force.

- Remove the flowers and store the essence in a dark amber stock bottle with equal amounts of brandy to preserve the mix and prevent the growth of any plant organisms.

Making Your Synergistic Flower Essences Blend

Dosage bottles of flower essences are prepared from a stock bottle—whether your own homemade stock bottle or the small stock bottles of Bach and Australian Bush Flower Essences that you have purchased. Generally, all flower essence blends are prepared by adding drops of essence to a dosage bottle of brandy and water, and this basic technique is applied with the synergistic essence blends.

Synergistic essence blends are often blended as combined flower and crystal essences, but this is not necessary. If you prefer, blend the two flower essences into a dosage bottle and take them separately from the crystal essence. Instructions for preparing a flower essences blend and combined essences blend are given; choose that which suits you best.

I am aware that many readers may be used to simply purchasing flower essences and taking them directly from the retail stock bottles; if you wish to take the Bach and Australian Bush Flower Essences separately, and your crystal essence, feel free to do so. Keep it simple. This is a life-enhancing practice, not one that should become a chore.

How to Prepare Your Synergistic Flower Essences Blend

- Fill a twenty-five milliliter amber dropper bottle with one quarter brandy and three-quarters pure spring water.

- Place three drops of the appropriate Bach Flower Essence and seven drops of the Australian Bush Flower Essence into the bottle.

- Replace the dropper cap and shake vigorously to blend and activate.

How to Prepare Your Combined Synergistic Flower and Crystal Essences Blend

- Fill a twenty-five milliliter amber dropper bottle with the prepared crystal essence as per the earlier instructions. The crystal essence replaces the brandy-spring water mix above.

- Place three drops of the appropriate Bach Flower Essence and seven drops of the Australian Bush Flower Essence into the crystal essence bottle.

- Replace the dropper cap and shake vigorously to blend and activate.

The usual dosage for the combined flower essences blend, crystal essence, or combined flower and crystal essences blend is four drops under the tongue, four times daily—or seven drops twice daily if your schedule is tight. Please take the first dose upon rising, and the last dose just before bed.

These powerful healers are totally safe, will do no harm, and are easily obtainable. The action is subtle but undeniably effective, and often unnoticed until healing is realized with a sense of wellness and well-being.

Spirit Connection

There is a power that is greater than us, a life force that flows through all living things, and from which all energy emanates—Source, Creator, Universal Mind, All That Is, God, Mother-Father God, Goddess/God, Allah, Yahweh, the I Am presence—is real!

Whether you relate to Higher Self, aspects of Divinity, or the unified field of pure potentialities, whatever your deity of choice, whatever aspect of Divinity you honor, I too honor and respect that. I relate to Spirit in all of her glorious guises; my connection is personal and nothing here is intended to counter your personal interpretation and knowing.

Your Higher Guidance

Our higher guidance is our Higher Self, our own Divinity. It is innate in each of us, part of the package when we come forth. The Higher Self or Inner Being is that part of us that is Divine, always connected to All That Is. There is no separation from the Universal field that links us all. Choosing from Higher Self is choosing from our own internal guidance system, that which guides us from a place of unconditional love; it is constant and consistent.

When we live a life inspired by Higher Self or higher guidance, we become aware that we always have a choice, and by pausing for a moment to see how the various options feel inside, we allow our Higher Self, our intuition to guide us in a way that will serve us well and serve the highest good of all concerned. We always have a choice ... and choosing to do nothing often serves the higher purpose. Choosing to embrace the synergistic combinations and practices as part of my daily routine has facilitated my connection to higher guidance and it is a connection that serves me joyously well.

Archangels and Angels

The word *angel* means messenger. Archangels are aspects of Divinity with specialized focus; they are light beings, pure vibration; they are celestial messengers and Spirit guides.

The synergistic combinations enhance resonance with specific archangels based purely on the highest harmonious vibration, which I determined by using the synergistic combination and immersing myself in the practice, and by subsequently blind-testing lists of archangels with my crystal pendulum. The results were consistently clear and incontrovertible. Many match crystals with archangel halo colors; the connections I am sharing are not intended to counter that work, but simply add to the body of knowledge we are amassing on the human journey.

I do not advocate absolutes in this world of glorious shadows and shades, and any gift from the Earth will resonate with Divine life-force energy and connect with higher guidance. Awareness of archangels is not vital to the synergistic practices—it is a choice. Some who have been dismissive of archangels have found that exploring the synergistic practices, being open and aware, gifted them guidance so nurturing, protective, and supportive that wonder and appreciation replaced cynicism. Archangelic vibration is constant; it is an aspect of Divinity, All That Is.

Those who enjoy working with archangels will find the combinations greatly enhance connection. Embracing regular daily practice lifts our vibration; as we evolve we lift our vibration; and sometimes we glimpse their fine vibration as we walk in fields of wonder.

Your Personal Guides and Teachers

Any aspect of Spirit that comes forth in connection with the synergistic practice is your personal guide or teacher. Spirit guides and teachers can include all aspects of Divinity, deities and celestial guides across time and space, or someone you have been personally connected to in the physical world, whose Spirit continues to support and guide you.

Some find connection with Spirit guides unclear, as if the line is full of interference. The synergy of these combinations is particularly helpful and, I believe, the clarity and ease with which the archangels come forth facilitates connection with guides and teachers. Working with our celestial guides and teachers is very different to archangels: these beings of Divinity can be uncompromising, playful, lovingly demanding, protective, and nurturing; they also express any number of other human characteristics and personalities.

·············

Connection to Spirit is deeply personal; if my words do not resonate with you, please continue to enjoy that which does. There is no separation, and our connection to Spirit is constant, whether through feeling grounded as we go about our day, supported by Mother Earth, guided by our own innate intuition, or connected to Higher Self or some celestial messenger. All are aspects of All That Is, Oneness, and we are blessed with abundance from which to choose.

Higher guidance connects with us through our feelings: inspired sight, thoughts, knowing, words, sounds, and visceral feelings that ripple through us. It is up to us to choose awareness of it; we get to choose how we live, self-responsibility and self-determination are always primary. But life that embraces Spirit can be sweet, and the flow slow and easy or speedy and exhilarating, or both, as we choose.

Bringing It All Together in a Daily Practice

And so, how do we bring it all together? As you know by now, I do not embrace a world of absolutes and for me there is no right or wrong way to enjoy these gifts from the Earth and Beyond—the magic is always in the combined practice. I believe the highest purpose would best be served, here, if I shared how I enjoy and embrace these synergistic combinations, which now form an integral part of my daily life. Please take from the following that which you feel would serve you well, or allow it to stimulate alternate practices that would best suit you.

I do suggest that you work with no more than two synergistic combinations, particularly at first, as too many only serves to confuse and overwhelm your entire being; this is a self-nurturing, self-supporting, and self-empowering practice, and confusion does not serve us well. Issues arise for us daily and are ever-changing as we evolve. If you feel overwhelmed by options, focus on key issues, remembering that as major issues are released and there is a shift toward alignment, other minor problems also change.

I have begun my day with meditation for many years, long before these synergistic combinations emerged. My day still begins with meditation, but as soon as my feet hit the floor in the morning, I internally ask which crystal or crystals would serve me well for that day. A collection of crystals sits constantly on my bedside table. I feel higher guidance as a ripple of awareness through me, or viscerally as a gut reaction, or in my heart and hands, or as a voice in my head; but as you now know, I most often use a crystal pendulum to dowse over the collection for speed and clarity of choice. The chosen stone or stones might remain current for hours, days, or more, but each morning I ask again, just to be sure. I always trust my higher guidance.

My crystals are always cleared with the appropriate essential oil (as you'll see in Part Two) and programmed to always work and guide me for the highest good. I then place four drops of the matching combined flower and crystal essences blend under my tongue, and I vaporize the appropriate essential oil (that was also used to clear my crystal) in my aromatherapy oil burner or diffuser as I meditate. If I am using two crystals then each is anointed with its appropriate oil, both oils are vaporized, and the essence blends for both crystals are taken. This is always about the synergy—whether it is synergy inherent in each combination, or the synergy that flows from two crystal combinations together.

As I sit with the anointed stone, essences, and aroma I feel deep appreciation and gratitude for the higher guidance and Spirit connection that I know is enhanced by the synergistic combination that will support me for the day. I know and trust that the awareness of Spirit will be that which I require, but if there is an aspect of Divinity I wish to call in, I will.

I hold the crystals in my cupped hands, as described in the meditations in Part Two. This connects my whole vibrational body with the energy vibrating from the crystal, the essential oil, and the flower and crystal essences—we become one vibrational energy system, connected to the infinite expansive energy of the Universe.

If at any time I feel a need for a particular healing, I might lie down and place the stone on the appropriate place on my body. For instance, recently I could feel a potential bout of conjunctivitis from too much screen work; one of the stones for the day was fluorite, so I took a break and lay flat on my back with the stone on the problem eye. I had been inspired that morning

to choose fluorite, which can treat skin and membrane infections and resonates with the great healing archangel, Raphael—moments like this bring
me such moments of wonder at the simple perfection of it all. The healing
buzz of the fluorite was immediate and a short time later, all was well.

The crystals stay with me for the day: either worn in a spiral cage necklace
at the heart or throat center, or in my pockets, or even tucked into my bra (in
this case, polished flat stones only!). They are there for me; they are there for
others as they radiate energy from me, or for me to use if someone is in need
of unexpected care—and of course the perfect stone is always with me. I place
a few drops of the essential oil, or oils, on a tissue or handkerchief to inhale as
I wish, and of course the essence blends are taken during the day. The essential
oil massage blend often serves as a moisturizer for the lower arms and legs.

As I mentioned, a collection of prepared crystals sits on my bedside table
and I am eternally aware and in gratitude of the healing and realigning that
takes place as I sleep—and I sleep exceptionally well! However, what we are
talking about, here, is the enhancement of the crystal that occurs when particular stones are overlaid with crystal essences and the highest harmonious
resonance of essential oils, combined flower essences, and higher guidance,
and the wellness and well-being that is facilitated. Each uplifts and enhances
the other; there is synergy in the combination.

There is a power greater than all of us, a life force that flows through us,
and bringing together these gifts from Mother Earth and Beyond facilitates us
being *however* we choose to be, and then being *all* that we choose to be. These
synergistic combinations can nourish us, sustain us, nurture us, support us,
empower us, and enhance our very being, if we so choose.

PART TWO

———

Synergistic Crystal Combinations and Practices

Amethyst

Traditional Chakra Association
Third Eye (6th) • Crown (7th)

Main Applications
Understanding • Trust • Connection • Forgiveness

Synergistic Combination
Crystal: Amethyst
Essential Oil: Lavender
Flower Essences: Cerato and Bluebell
Archangel: Zadkiel

Amethyst vibrates with energies that are powerful, protecting, and healing and has been used back through the mists of time. The Egyptians used it to guard against feeling negative, guilty, and fearful. Amethyst has long been used for protection on all levels—against self-deception as it enhances our wisdom and knowing, and against psychic attack and witchcraft; it also has a long association with royalty and rulers, bringing strength and prosperity. Amethyst symbolizes spiritual wisdom, humility, faith, and sincerity.

Long recognized as offering a vibration that opens the spiritual and psychic centers, it is known as a power stone. Wearing an amethyst necklace, or holding a stone, offers powerful support for meditation as it opens and activates the crown chakra, and stimulates the third eye, therefore enhancing connection to Spirit and helping maintain the meditative state—it soothes the mind, focuses the attention, and brings a deep sense of serenity.

We have now entered the Aquarian Age and many see amethyst as the perfect symbol of this Age. This highly spiritual stone resonates to balance the physical, mental, and emotional bodies, bringing contentment, strength, and peace.

Jewelry that combines amethyst with silver is often favored by healers—it unites the spiritual and physical world as we go about our daily lives, and has the power to focus the healer's energy. Wearing amethyst not only empowers through connection to Spirit, but also powerfully protects and shields against negative energies.

Amethyst crystal clusters are useful in the home to maintain a positive clean flow of life force through the house—a group of tumbled stones or clusters on a sunny windowsill are highly beneficial to heal any negativity in the home. Alternatively, stones placed in the moonlight will help calm everyone in the home.

How Amethyst Facilitates Well-Being

- Amethyst is uplifting, positive, and highly spiritual and balances the physical, mental, and emotional bodies bringing contentment, strength, and peace.

- It is a powerful aid to meditation—but also unites the spiritual and the physical as we go about our day-to-day life.

- Placed under the pillow, amethyst is used as a dream stone to generate healing and prophetic dreams.

- Amethyst can calm the storm—it will prevent, or stimulate, a release of guilt and negative thoughts as required.

- When feeling stressed, if we are willing to take a moment to hold a stone in the non-dominant hand and allow the energy to flow, the calming, soothing vibrations can penetrate our very being to bring a sense of peace and serenity.

- Self-awareness and a preparedness to take responsibility for self are enhanced.

- Creativity is stimulated, as is the ability to join the threads of new ideas and reason and think through ideas with spiritual insight and clarity of intuition.

- Amethyst vibrates to release energy blockages within the body and the aura, and the stone is able to dissolve and transmute negative thoughts and energies to be redistributed for the highest good.

The amethyst synergistic combination may be a new creation for me, but some of the components have been with me for most of my life—constantly and consistently vibrating their magic energy, clearing space, enhancing clarity and awareness of opportunity, and facilitating understanding and supporting my curiosity. I was still a teenager when my mother gifted me a magnificent piece of amethyst, which she had bought while traveling through Central Australia, the Outback.

This was my first crystal—this was my *only* crystal for many decades. My decision to formally embrace, study, and practice natural therapies and dance with Spirit followed half a lifetime of choices that bear little resemblance to my life today. This piece of amethyst has left home with me, watched me party with friends, awaited my many returns while I traveled overseas, adorned the mantel of my first "renovator's delight" real estate purchase, and watched me dress for my wedding. In fact, she was still there on another mantel shelf as we finally decided to simplify and change our lives with a move from the city to the country in the final years just before the new millennium. She's been there through the highs and the lows, and holds in her glittering purple points the memory of all those moments of awareness and change, joy and wonder, and all those moments I'd rather forget, and probably many I have not remembered. This purple beauty has been a constant in my life and, I feel no doubt, now holds my mother's beautiful energy as well as that of Mother Earth.

This amethyst synergistic combination is one I turn to in even the smallest of moments when I feel fragmented and unsure, or overwhelmed, anxious, and unclear. Once I decide to take some quiet time, use the combined essences, inhale the familiar uplifting floral aroma, sit with the amethyst, and invite in the guidance the synergy facilitates, peace and calmness quickly flow through me, and understanding and clarity unfold.

Essential Oils, Flower Essences, and Spirit Connection

Amethyst is a much-loved stone and a great healer, but its potential broadens immeasurably if used in concert with other life-enhancing gifts. When we treat ourselves to the synergy in specific combinations, we then allow ourselves to be surprised and delighted by the transformation that flows from awareness, connection, and trust.

Essential Oils

Lavender is regularly recommended with amethyst and for good reason! The highest resonance is between amethyst and lavender essential oil. Traditionally, amethyst is placed at the third eye and crown chakras, but this power combination will work effectively and synergistically to harmonize the whole being whether the crystal is placed on the body, held, worn, carried in the pocket, or placed nearby.

Calming and relaxing lavender (*Lavandula angustifolia*) has been used for centuries both as a perfume and a medicinal herb—the name comes from the Latin *lavare* meaning "to wash" and, today, it is often regarded as "first aid in a bottle." Lavender essential oil is distilled from flower heads and leaves; it complements most oils and gives a subtle floral and soothing quality to any mixture.

Its antiseptic properties make it excellent for applying to burns and wounds, and a lavender oil solution was used as a surgical antiseptic in early field hospitals. Apart from its extensive properties applicable to the body physical, lavender essential oil will also detoxify chemicals and metallics from the air, and its uplifting harmonizing aroma stimulates an emotional response, thus helping to release emotional trauma.

The uplifting mauve magic of lavender calms agitation, anger, obsession, and panic; settles and balances mood swings and restlessness; uplifts boredom, sorrow, and grief; and stimulates and focuses poor concentration and daydreaming so that ideas can be realized.

Lavender really is one of the great relaxers—the great leveler that reduces stress and calms the nervous system, restoring homeostasis, our body's innate equilibrium and balance. Its gentle, soft fragrance creates calm and order from chaos, and it harmonizes and balances every aspect of the body, mind, and spirit. A few drops of lavender is wonderful for insomnia as tension is relieved and sleep induced; a few drops massaged down the spine of an overactive child is likewise helpful at bedtime. Lavender is the perfect base for any stress-relief blend—while neroli is considered specific for stress, lavender and neroli make a wonderfully soothing stress blend. Neroli is discussed with fluorite, quartz, and selenite synergistic combinations.

On the emotional barometer, lavender aligns with the spiritual body and can transform the negative feeling of neglected into nurtured. Nurturing begins with self, and lavender brings expansive awareness and understanding that only through nurturing ourselves do we open our ability to nurture others—and to be nurtured by fellow travelers along the way. What a wonderfully transformative gift that is!

Lavender essential oil is an old favorite that I'm sure was enjoyed by many across generations. My maternal grandmother was a keen gardener, the daughter of a quiet gentle orchardist who taught her to "tickle the soil so the plants will grow," and mauve abundance bordered extensive strawberry gardens thick with plants drooping with lush red berries.

My mother grew long borders of lavender at our family home and, after my husband Gary and I left the city, lovely lavender was the first herb I cut, bunched, and dried from the rafters of the old corrugated-iron hay shed that had been standing in the back paddock for more than half a century. This much-loved mauve beauty has, likewise, been a constant as I have shifted and changed, grown and evolved, over the years—the fragrance today no less pleasing and calming than when I first smelled the crushed flowers from my grandmother's hand.

Flower Essences

The highest resonance is between amethyst and Cerato Bach Flower and Bluebell Australian Bush Flower Essences.

Cerato is the Bach Flower Essence when we doubt our own judgment to the point where we continually seek advice from others and lose the ability to discern and discriminate and trust our own decisions—in other words, we often doubt what feels right to us. It relates to our inner voice, that which gives an inner sense of certainty.

The negative Cerato type is often unaware they are allowing themselves to be overly influenced by the opinions of others, but then become dis-Spirited when things turn out poorly as they instinctively knew they would. Indeed, there is a disconnect between the intuitive heartfelt response or gut instinct where we feel intuitively what the best choice would be for us and the rational brain that kicks in with mental arguments backed up by entrenched behavior patterns and core beliefs.

The negative Cerato type loves to take opinion polls or "doctor shop" until they hear what they want to hear. There is a complete lack of self-responsibility and self-belief—an abdication of their own self-power that will innately guide them, protect them, and sustain them in the best way possible.

The possible Cerato transformation is the faith to take one day at a time with quiet self-assurance and self-belief in their own capability. Intuition is heightened, connection is strengthened, and self-responsibility and self-determination are embraced. Dreams often seem stimulated with Cerato, which greatly enhances our ability to remember dreams more coherently and in a more meaningful way, further supporting our trust in the heightened intuition. Once Cerato types embrace their powerful intuition, their innate wisdom and understanding is restored bringing quiet self-assurance.

Bluebell is the Australian Bush Flower Essence for those who have closed off from their emotions and feelings, their innate guidance; they become rigid, unbending, and unadaptable; they sink into feelings of lack on all levels and feel a need to grip tightly whatever joys they hold. Bluebell was sourced from the Olgas in Australia, a powerful spiritual center of the Land Down Under, and taps into this unconscious fear that there is not enough.

Our emotions are always an integral part of us, but sometimes painful events, traumas, or triggers cause us to shut down and cut ourselves off from our feelings to protect ourselves. We hold the joyful emotions tight within and seek to control our environment in case we lose the cherished feelings of love and joy that cannot be replaced.

The potential Bluebell transformation brings trust that all is indeed well; there is a shift that opens the heart to the innate abundance in All That Is and a desire to joyfully participate, engage, and share that which is available to each of us. Love is no longer conditional; joy and abundance are no longer finite; life is no longer a struggle or a competition with others. We return to balance and the assurance that as we give, we receive, and as we receive, we give—we flow with the infinite current of "well-beingness" as we travel the wondrous river of life.

Archangels

The highest resonance is between amethyst and Archangel Zadkiel.

Zadkiel is the archangel of forgiveness, mercy, benevolence, and unconditional kindness and compassion. He teaches us to shift our perception and show more mercy, compassion, gentleness, and kindness to ourselves and to others; we serve the highest good when we lower our guard with ourselves (and with others), and embrace our own innate connection and guidance, and our connection with others. There are no accidents; there are gifts in each interaction, connection, and moment.

Opportunities for compassion, non-judgment and forgiveness often coalesce when those from the past once again come into our lives—our lack of judgment, forgiveness for what may or may not have happened in the past, and unconditional kindness contribute to a powerful energetic shift into a more peaceful and accepting environment for all.

Zadkiel also enhances memory and is often recommended to students to call on during exams. However, his combined focus of memory and forgiveness brings a powerful opportunity to clear past pain and hurt and anger, which if not released only serve to inhibit us going forward and fulfilling our potential. Zadkiel offers powerful support as we release judgment and negativity, which opens us up to forgiveness and compassion toward self and others; he works with Archangel Michael to clear negative energies and sweep clean each layer of our being when we decide to willingly and lovingly release the negativity that does not serve us well.

We are encouraged to seek balance, to take a broader view of situations, and to change any negative perceptions to ones that serve us, not hinder us. Forgiveness, kindness, and compassion to self and others are fundamental to us fulfilling our potential and manifesting our dreams.

At our deepest essence, we are Spirit, and Zadkiel helps us to reconnect and remember that which we are, and so self-esteem, self-worth, and self-awareness are strengthened to go forward. We feel empowered and protected to forgive and let go, embrace kindness and compassion, and appreciate the wisdom and understanding that flows to us and from us.

....

I have personally enjoyed Zadkiel's energetic brush dislodging and sweeping away residual negativity from the body. Experience has shown me the powerful release and cleansing that we are gifted when we choose to lovingly and willingly release old or new negative energies with the support of this amethyst synergistic combination. I have been gifted wondrous clarity, awareness, appreciation, and understanding and decisiveness; I have been gifted awareness of connection; I have been gifted quiet self-assurance that I'm doing okay and am perfect in all of my imperfections; and my fire of creativity, passion for the wonder of life, and curiosity to explore some more are reignited.

Finally, and most importantly, forgiveness is always facilitated—forgiveness of self and others—for which I express my heartfelt gratitude and appreciation. Forgiveness opens doors previously unseen by us; forgiveness brings deep inner peace, clarity, and awareness; forgiveness is the greatest gift we give ourselves, and we deserve no less.

Meditation Practices

By choosing to quiet the mind with the amethyst synergistic combination we open up to our innate connection to Spirit and the gifts of understanding, trust, and forgiveness that connection brings, as the physical integrates with the spiritual, through the mental and emotional bodies. We embrace a sense of wonder at the innate order, balance, and perfection in it all. The infinite field of possibilities and potentialities is there for each of us. There is an elusive richness to a life that is regularly refreshed and aligned by quiet time alone in contemplation.

For the following meditations, please have at hand your crystal, essential oil, and crystal and flower essences. The crystal essence and combined flower essences may be taken in a single blend or used separately, whichever is most convenient to you. The essential oil may certainly be vaporized in an oil burner to fill the meditation space, but as this is not always doable or convenient in some locations, please be assured that a few drops of essential oil on a tissue or handkerchief will serve you well at any time or place—whether meditating at home or in the park, or simply connecting while in line at the supermarket.

Sit in whatever way is comfortable for you—if seated in a chair, have your feet flat on the floor with no shoes. Ensure your back is straight by gently lifting your heart center. Relax your shoulders. Lengthen the back of the neck by slightly tilting the chin downward.

Take a couple of breaths and bring yourself to a place of quiet appreciation of this time that you are gifting you.

Meditation to Connect with the Amethyst Synergy

This is perhaps the simplest and "earthiest" of the three meditations using this synergystic combination. In this meditation, we connect to the high vibrational energy that is created by the specific combination of these gifts from Mother Earth: amethyst stone, lavender essential oil, and a blend of amethyst, Cerato, and Bluebell essences. As always, it is all about the synergy of the combination. I use this meditation whenever I feel in need of the support, clarity, and understanding that inevitably follow as I am calmed and uplifted. To connect with the amethyst synergy, you will need:

Amethyst crystal

Lavender essential oil

Cerato and Bluebell flower essences

Amethyst crystal essence

- Place four drops of the combined Cerato and Bluebell flower essences and amethyst crystal essence under your tongue. Take a breath.

- Anoint the amethyst with a drop of lavender essential oil. Inhale the uplifting floral fragrance as you gently rub the oil into the stone, breathing slowly and deeply. Take a breath.

- Cup the amethyst lightly in your hands—the fingertips of the right hand gently touch to the base of the left palm— and rest your hands comfortably in your lap. Take a breath and softly close your eyes.

- Feel the energy of the amethyst as it fills your cupped hands— for example, it may feel tingling, effervescent, light, heavy, or like your hands are suctioned together or they may expand apart during the session—there is no right way it should feel, and how it feels is right for you.

- Feel or imagine the energy moving up through your arms, through to the heart center, and radiating out to fill your being in whatever way feels right for you.

- Thoughts will come and go; let them. Trust that the synergy of the combination will stimulate, calm, heal, open, or enhance that which needs attention at this time.

- You may see the mauve purple of the amethyst behind the closed eyes—maybe glittering flashes, maybe an expansive mist or swirls of color, or deep color that fades in and out, as the energy of the amethyst combination connects with various energy centers.

- Feel gratitude for any understanding, clarity, or awareness that comes to you and let it go, trusting that it will be there for you when you come out of the meditation.

- Feel the energy. Be in wonder of the synergy of these combined gifts from Mother Earth. Luxuriate in the connection; allow it to fill you and nourish you and remain within that expansive grounded space for as long as you wish.

Meditation on the Essence of the Amethyst Combination (with Affirmations)

For me, this is the most powerful of the three amethyst meditations to support change, enhance understanding, and support a heartfelt decision to trust and let go of that which no longer serves us. Inner strength is enhanced and supported by connection and compassion. Again, it is all about the combination's synergy that lifts the vibration of our physical, emotional, mental, and spiritual bodies, and the specific affirmations are an integral component of the synergy of this meditation practice. The affirmations allow and facilitate change in ways that continually surprise and delight me—the words remain unchanged each time, but the results are as different as I am each time I change and grow, and then return to this inspired amethyst affirmation practice.

- Please sit in your comfortable meditation position.

- Place four drops of your combined Cerato and Bluebell flower essences and amethyst crystal essence under the tongue, anoint your amethyst with a drop of lavender essential oil and inhale a few drops of lavender from a tissue or handkerchief while holding your stone in lightly cupped hands.

- Settle into the position, close your eyes, and take a long, slow, deep breath, releasing any tension on the exhale. Repeat with two more breaths.

- Take your awareness behind the eyebrow center. This is the third eye chakra. The color is deep indigo or purple. See yourself sitting in the middle of this space—the one in the middle who intuitively knows.

- Breathe.

- Take your awareness to the crown above you. See it layered with the petals of a closed lotus flower and imagine those petals unfolding, opening to pure positive energy and the infinite field of possibilities.

- Allow the pure white light to illuminate and enliven the deep indigo purple of this space. Feel the energy flood in and cascade through the physical body.

- Breathe.

- Repeat this statement to yourself. *I am gifted wisdom and understanding.*

- Breathe.

- Take your awareness to just below the navel center. This is the sacral chakra. The color is a rich orange. See the pelvic area as a golden bowl filled with the vibrant orange waters of creativity. You sit in the middle on a giant lotus leaf, perfectly balanced, fully supported.

- Breathe.

- No matter which way you choose to move, the liquid always returns to balance with you perfectly supported in the middle.

- Breathe.

- Repeat this statement to yourself. *I am gifted trust.*

- Breathe.

- Take your awareness to the chest center. This is the heart chakra—the middle chakra, that which bridges the upper three and lower three. The color is vibrant emerald or forest green. See yourself in the middle on a vibrant pink and white lotus flower atop a green lotus leaf. You are seated in your heart, the center of unconditional love.

- Breathe.

- See the heart center flooded with Divine energy from above as life-force energy rises to meet it from below. You are supported in Love from above and below.

- Repeat this statement to yourself. *I am gifted connection... there is no separation, and I am forgiven.*

- Breathe.

- This powerful energy from your heart center floods down your arms and out through your hands to touch the world. You are fully supported and in your power as you choose to act from your heart.

- Repeat the full affirmation, feeling Spirit, or your innate Divinity, Higher Self, or beautiful Inner Being speaking to you. *You are gifted wisdom and understanding, and trust. You are gifted connection... there is no separation, and you are forgiven. You are energy being human.*

- Breathe. Remain in this space, feeling this space, for as long as it feels comfortable, or as long as your schedule allows.

- When you are ready, take a deep breath and bring your awareness back to the crown. See the petals of the lotus flower closing once again—yours to open at will, and close at will.

- Take another long, slow breath.

- Bring your awareness back into the body. Wiggle your toes and fingers, gently move your hands and your head, and open your eyes to bring your awareness fully back into this moment.

- Express gratitude for All That Is and the gift of grace … and be aware that your Source is even more grateful for all that you are, and all that you are becoming. And so It is.

Meditation to Connect with Archangel Zadkiel, Higher Self, and Spirit Guides and Teachers

This simple meditation is often favored by those who already enjoy working with archangels, Spirit, guides, or teachers, but please remember that they are all aspects of our innate Divinity or essence. Whether you wish to connect with the energy of Archangel Zadkiel for support or energetic clearing of low vibrational energy that is limiting you, or whether you wish to connect to your own Inner Being, the synergy of the amethyst combination will powerfully support your heartfelt intention to be present in the moment and to be open to allow that which is there for you to flow to you.

- Please sit in your comfortable meditation position.

- If you have a question or a situation with which you would like clarity or guiding support, bring that to mind.

- If you have a favorite invocation or preferred ritual for connecting to your teachers, guides, or Spirit, please use that which feels right for you.

- Place four drops of your combined Cerato and Bluebell flower essences and amethyst crystal essence under the tongue, anoint your amethyst with a drop of lavender essential oil, inhale a few drops of the calming and nurturing lavender oil from a tissue or handkerchief and throughout the meditation if you feel inspired to do so, and hold your stone in lightly cupped hands.

- Settle into the position, close your eyes, and take a long, slow, deep breath, releasing any tension on the exhale. Repeat with two more breaths.

- Feeling relaxed, still, and present to the moment, please state your intentions. *I am present for all that is here for me. I am listening, and you are welcome.*

- Breathe and release any tension with a long exhalation.

- The soft sound of the breath mirrors the tranquil space of silence where inner peace and harmony are found. Feel the breath, hear the breath, and allow for any awareness of connection that follows.

- Feel deep appreciation and gratitude for this time of connection to a Divine messenger, teacher, or aspect of Oneness, and come out of the meditation whenever you are ready.

Please know that no matter what you feel or do not feel during the meditation, any question you have asked has been answered, any clarity you are seeking has been forthcoming, and any connection you desired has been facilitated by the synergy of the high vibrational combination of amethyst crystal, lavender essential oil, the amethyst, Cerato and Bluebell essence blend, and Archangel Zadkiel. Your conscious awareness of understanding, trust, your innate connection, and the powerful gift of forgiveness have been awakened and heightened. If this is not a familiar practice for you, please be reassured that enhanced connection is always facilitated and clarity and answers always provided. Sometimes guidance will flow into your consciousness during the practice, sometimes you will be inspired to pick up a particular book, or turn onto a certain radio or television channel, or bump into someone as you go about your day. The answers and clarity always flow, but we do not always get to micromanage how they come to us. Indeed, trusting in our inherent guidance will always deliver that which we seek in the quickest, most direct, and life-enhancing way ... we just need to trust.

Remember, it is in the smallest of moments that miracles happen and the healing forgiveness and awakening of Zadkiel and associated teachers and guides, including your Higher Self, facilitated through the synergy of the amethyst combination is indeed inspired.

Aquamarine

TRADITIONAL CHAKRA ASSOCIATION
Throat (5th) • Third Eye (6th)

MAIN APPLICATIONS
Speaking Truth • Grace • Harmony
Being One's Own True North

SYNERGISTIC COMBINATION
Crystal: Aquamarine
Essential Oil: Lemongrass
Flower Essences: Star of Bethlehem
and Slender Rice Flower
Archangel: Jophiel

The beautiful pale green-blue aquamarine is often called Water of the Sea, and has been used since the ancients as a stone of protection, courage, and harmony. The ancient Greeks and Romans revered it as protection for sailors to bring them safe passage and bountiful success as they voyaged across the seas, and the ancient Egyptians and other Middle Eastern cultures also valued this stone of protection and purity. Aquamarine was also valued in many cultures for protection against gossip.

Aquamarine harmonizes and resonates with the throat chakra, our center of communication and purification. It encourages expression of one's own truth: we find courage to speak our truth, with clarity and purity, to ourselves and to the world; we speak with grace, nothing to prove and nothing to de-fend; and we feel strong and protected, able to discern and discriminate when and where we choose to speak our truth—discriminating choice empowers self-determination as we stand authentically in our own truth. We become our own moral compass.

The soft beauty of aquamarine should not be underestimated: it is a stone of power and courage, and powerfully protects and shields the auric bodies, every layer of our being. It is also healing as it calms, soothes, re-duces stress, and harmonizes internal and external environments—it has a particular affinity with the mental, emotional, and spiritual bodies of those who are more sensitive.

An aquamarine necklace is soothing to wear and further protects the physical body by stimulating the thymus gland and therefore the body's self-protecting and self-healing mechanism: the immune system.

Lying down to meditate with aquamarine on the third eye, aventurine at the heart chakra and citrine on the Hara, or sacral chakra, can facilitate a won-derful emotional healing that balances the physical experience with Higher Self and Spirit.

Aquamarine is a powerful aid to deep meditation, bringing a profound sense of peace and tranquility, and enhancing our connection with Spirit, our Higher Self, or our Inner Being—we access the wisdom of the soul. Those who are practiced in meditation have reportedly received wisdom, and expe-rienced a connection to Oneness, when meditating on an aquamarine. This beautiful water-like stone enhances our center of creativity and our ability to flow through life, to float on the river of life, enjoying safe passage and courage to explore, and feeling clear on where we are heading.

How Aquamarine Facilitates Well-Being

- Aquamarine calms the mind and is excellent for enhancing perception and how we choose to view that which happens around us.

- It helps overcome entrenched beliefs and choices that are self-defeating and self-sabotaging—we are empowered to stop running the same old program.

- Aquamarine helps us maintain smooth communication and is often recommended as the perfect choice for partners to exchange.

- This wonderful meditation stone raises spiritual awareness, often with a sense of giving and service, and facilitates higher consciousness.

- Aquamarine also enhances connection to our innate intuition and internal guidance.

Knowing that I am being, and I am, my own true north is hugely self-empowering. In the past, I have regularly dived straight into negativity and struggle, and often scraped the bottom of the pond to stir up old self-doubt and self-worthiness issues.

Today, I need only stand in my truth, knowing my true north is ever constant—my truth evolves as I learn, integrate, and grow; and from each new place I learn, integrate, and grow. Integration is the key—we must integrate what we choose to take on board and leave behind that which does not feel right for us. Life does not have to be a struggle, and it can change whenever we choose to view ourselves and events from a broader perspective.

This aquamarine synergistic combination can quickly help me return to balance when I feel I have floated in a slipstream into dark water that feels troubling: I am supported as I pause, look around, feel if I wish to stay and explore, whether I can be of service, whether there is something here for me to experience, or whether I need to simply allow my true north to bring me back to where I choose to be at this time in my life.

When I speak my truth, it is with discernment and discrimination. I have no need or intention to convince or defend, simply to share. When I speak my truth from my own true north, I speak with grace and with a sense of harmony and respect for all. Aquamarine synergistic combination certainly helps me find, and be, my own true north. There is, indeed, great beauty there.

Essential Oils, Flower Essences, and Spirit Connection

Aquamarine benefits our being very well on its own, but those benefits are expanded to bring unimagined versatility when used in combination. The synergy of the following combinations encourages a sense of expansiveness and wonder that will encourage and delight as you navigate your way forward.

Essential Oils

Roman chamomile has been cited by some practitioners as resonating well with aquamarine at the throat chakra, and the colors certainly make sense. However, the highest resonance is between aquamarine and lemongrass essential oil. Traditionally, aquamarine is used with the throat and third eye chakras, but this power combination works effectively and synergistically to harmonize the whole being whether the crystal is placed on the body, held, worn, carried in the pocket, or placed nearby.

Lemongrass will be a familiar culinary delight to all lovers of Asian cuisine and flavors—the fleshy white stem bases are eaten and the leaves are used for oil. Lemongrass (*Cymbopogon citratus*) essential oil is distilled from the tough inedible leaves, which release their intense herby lemon fragrance when crushed or bruised.

Lemongrass is arousing, mood uplifting, reviving, revitalizing, stimulating, calming, stress-reducing, pain-reducing, antidepressant, balancing to the nervous system, and sleep promoting. It opens the physical body to the Divine life-force energy of the breath, and tonifies and harmonizes the subtle bodies. The radiant energy of lemongrass aroma is purifying and inspirational to every level of our being.

On the emotional barometer, lemongrass resonates particularly with the mental body, transforming negative feelings of restriction and limitation into that of expansion. We are able to experience the wonder of life, aware of the infinite field of possibilities and potentialities available to us all, and appreciate that belief in the impossible is a self-imposed limitation. We feel inspired and uplifted; we are fascinated by the prospects; our spirits are lifted by Spirit; we feel motivated to engage with All That Is and set sail to discover what's on offer feeling fully supported.

Feeling expansive and open allows us to be authentic. We feel the breath supporting us and opening us up to the unlimited possibilities around us when we stand in our integrity and choose to live in the wonder of life.

Flower Essences

The highest resonance is between aquamarine and Star of Bethlehem Bach Flower and Slender Rice Flower Australian Bush Flower Essences.

Star of Bethlehem is possibly one of my most often used Bach Flower remedies in my clinic situation. Dr. Bach called Star of Bethlehem the "comforter and soother of pains and sorrows." It is the remedy for the effects of all kinds of shock and relates to the recalibration of the soul, reorientation to our true north, and awakening to all we know at a soul level.

Shock or trauma to our system can be acute or ongoing, current or long past, and it can be something of which we are consciously aware or something hardly noticed but, stored in the channels of the unconscious, it continues to radiate its unhelpful vibration years after the event. Indeed, events may be traced back to childhood and memories unconscious or repressed. Pain and trauma, whether physical, mental, or emotional, show up in the body physical in myriad different ways, but many are conditions induced by stress and/or nervous system imbalance including psychosomatic conditions that resist treatment. Few of us go through life unscathed by the impact of a traumatic event.

The potential Star of Bethlehem transformation is restoration of our inner vitality, clarity of mind, and inner strength as we reconnect with Higher Self. Residual negative energy can be dissolved and undone. Our innate balance is restored and strong, able to recover quickly from any negativity or trauma that strikes our being; our beautiful nervous system, ever sensitive to change, is now powerfully adaptable to any shifts and changes in energy in our internal or external environment.

Slender Rice Flower is the Australian Bush Flower Essence that relates to narrow-mindedness and holding restricted negative points of view, which are so limiting; there is perpetual negative judgment and comparison with others and feelings of jealousy or superiority.

These narrow viewpoints often stem from past events—the lack of tolerance and love for fellow man or particular groups of humanity are often handed down through generations and relate back to obscure events from the distant past. Those who give safe harbor to such restrictive views will often succumb to illness in the body physical.

The positive outcome is a more open and expansive view that enhances harmony and cooperation within self and within the group or community. Indeed the structure of Slender Rice Flower is one of many flowers clustered tightly together to form a perfect sphere-shape flower head—the perfect symbol of the unity of humanity.

Humility replaces pride, deeper understanding and appreciation replace narrow ignorance, cooperation replaces compliance, tolerance replaces intolerance, harmony replaces disharmony, and expansiveness replaces restriction in the individual, and so the group.

Archangels

The highest resonance is between aquamarine and Archangel Jophiel.

Archangel Jophiel helps us create and attract more beauty into our lives as we connect in to the Divine beauty of All That Is. We see and appreciate the beauty in every moment; our thoughts are uplifted as we open to our inner beauty. Some traditions regard Jophiel as a great archangel—companion of Archangel Metatron (see Moonstone), who is the Angel or Prince of Divine Presence; companion to Archangel Zadkiel (see Amethyst) assisting Archangel Michael (see Clear Quartz) in battle; and the spirit of Jupiter when it is in Sagittarius.

Jophiel helps us bring beauty into our lives on every level by encouraging us to see the splendor of the Divine Light radiating from within ourselves. We think and feel beauty when we stand in authenticity, in our own truth; from that place we feel uplifted about ourselves and the wider community. We think, speak, and act with the beauty that flows from Divine grace within.

We embrace self-awareness, self-realization, and self-responsibility to be true to ourselves and speak gently and clearly with ourselves and with others. We appreciate the gifts of grace, harmony, forgiveness, unconditional love, and healing that flow from choosing to live in integrity, to be authentic with our words and choices, and to live with appreciation and gratitude for all that is.

. . . .

Using the aquamarine synergistic blend, I have come to see our true north as that light of Divinity at our core, a beacon from which we can take our bearings and return back home, back into alignment with our true north when we stray too far off course.

I always know I am off course because it simply feels awful—at best I feel "a bit off"; at worst I speed down the slippery slope of fear into self-doubt and entrenched negative beliefs that, I guess, we all tend to revisit over a lifetime. I know there is no beauty to be found there.

Speaking our truth, embracing the notion that when we act from an inspired heart we are acting from own true north, are fundamental components of living in energetic integrity, of being authentic. What does this mean? It means we *feel* we are being true to Self—and that's the clue, we have to *feel* our way there.

Being true to ourselves, true to that which feels right for us, comes from inside of us, from our "feeling brain" low in the belly in the sacral chakra, the Hara, the Zen Knowing Mind, that which knows all, outside of time and space. Our heart sits halfway between our Hara and our third eye, our center of intuition and inspiration; our heart bridges the lower and higher chakras. Energy from the heart chakra extends down through our arms to our hands, with which we reach out to touch and embrace the world. When we act from our hearts, we act with grace, in harmony and balance; when we speak from our hearts, we speak with grace that flows from our true north, our core.

So how do I know if I am in tune, in sync with my own true north? I *feel* it ... and it feels wonderful—yes, full of wonder; it feels gentle yet powerful, compassionate, nourishing, nurturing, sustaining, and simply right for *all* concerned at that time. There is great beauty there; Divine grace is there.

Meditation Practices

By choosing to quiet the mind with this aquamarine synergistic combination we open to the gentle strength of our own truth which we speak with grace, harmony, and clarity, allowing it to integrate the physical with the spiritual, through the mental and emotional bodies. We embrace a sense of wonder at the innate order, balance, and perfection in it all as we connect with our own internal guidance and become our own true north. The infinite field of possibilities and potentialities is there for each of us. There is an elusive richness to a life that is regularly refreshed and aligned by quiet time alone in contemplation.

For the following meditations, please have at hand your crystal, essential oil, and crystal and flower essences. The crystal essence and combined flower essences may be taken in a single blend, or used separately, as is most convenient to you. The essential oil may certainly be vaporized in an oil burner to fill the meditation space, but as this is not always doable or convenient in some locations, please be assured that a few drops of essential oil on a tissue or handkerchief will serve you well at any time and in any location—whether meditating at home or on the beach, or simply connecting in while waiting in line at the ferry terminal.

Sit in whatever way is comfortable for you—if seated in a chair, have your feet flat on the floor with no shoes. Ensure your back is straight by gently lifting your heart center. Relax your shoulders. Lengthen the back of the neck by slightly tilting the chin downward.

Take a couple of breaths and bring yourself to a place of quiet appreciation of this time that you are gifting you.

Meditation to Connect with the Aquamarine Synergy

Some might feel that this is the least complicated and "earthiest" of the three meditations using this combination. In this meditation, we connect to the high vibrational energy that is created by the specific combination of these gifts from Mother Earth: aquamarine stone, lemongrass essential oil, and a blend of aquamarine, Star of Bethlehem, and Slender Rice Flower essences. As always, it is all about the synergy of the combination. I use this meditation whenever I feel in need of the harmony and strength that inevitably follow as I am calmed, inspired, and uplifted. To connect with the aquamarine synergy, you will need:

Aquamarine crystal

Lemongrass essential oil

Star of Bethlehem and Slender Rice Flower flower essences

Aquamarine crystal essence

- Place four drops of the combined Star of Bethlehem and Slender Rice Flower flower essences and aquamarine crystal essence under your tongue. Take a breath.

- Anoint the aquamarine with a drop of lemongrass essential oil. Inhale the inspiring and revitalizing aroma as you gently rub the oil into the stone, breathing slowly and deeply.

- Cup the aquamarine lightly in your hands—the fingertips of the right hand gently touch the base of the left palm—and rest your hands comfortably in your lap. Take a deep breath, softly close your eyes, and release with the exhalation.

- Feel the energy of the aquamarine as it fills your cupped hands—for example, it may feel tingling, effervescent, light, heavy, or like your hands are suctioned together or they may expand apart during the session—there is no right way it should feel, and how it feels is right for you.

- Feel or imagine the energy moving up through your arms, through to the heart center, and radiating out to fill your entire being in whatever way feels right for you.

- Know that the synergy of the combination will calm, heal, open, or enhance that which needs attention at this time.

- You may see the blue-green of the aquamarine behind the closed eyes—maybe flashes, maybe an expansive sea of color, or color that fades in and out, as the energy of the aquamarine combination connects with the your Inner Being and inner voice, and the various energy centers.

- Feel gratitude for any truth, direction, or guidance that comes to you and let it go, trusting that it has settled into your being and will be with you, guiding you and flowing through you when you come out of the meditation.

- Feel the energy. Be in wonder of the synergy of these combined gifts from Mother Earth. Luxuriate in the connection; feel the flow that supports you and allow it to fill you, nourish you, and sustain you. Remain within that expansive grounded space for as long as you wish.

Meditation on the Essence of the Aquamarine Combination (with Affirmations)

This is the most powerful aquamarine meditation for supporting change and a sincere decision to release all that limits us at any given time. We are strengthened to honor us and be in harmony with that which we truly are. Again, it is all about the synergy of the combination that lifts the vibration of our physical, emotional, mental, and spiritual bodies, and the specific affirmations are an integral component of the synergy of this meditation practice. The affirmations allow and facilitate change in ways that continually surprise and delight me—the words remain unchanged each time, but the results are as different as I am each time I change and grow, and then return to this inspired aquamarine affirmation practice.

- Please sit in your comfortable meditation position.

- Place four drops of your combined Star of Bethlehem and Slender Rice Flower flower essences and aquamarine crystal essence under the tongue, anoint your aquamarine with a drop of lemongrass essential oil, and inhale a few drops of lemongrass from a tissue or handkerchief while holding your stone in lightly cupped hands.

- Settle into the position, close your eyes, and take a long, slow, deep breath, releasing any tension on the exhale. Repeat with two more breaths.

- Take your awareness behind the eyebrow center. This is the third eye chakra. The color is deep indigo or purple. See yourself sitting in the middle of this space—the one in the middle who intuitively knows.

- Breathe.

- Take your awareness to the crown above you. See it layered with the petals of a closed lotus flower and imagine those petals unfolding, opening to pure positive energy and the infinite field of possibilities.

- Allow the pure white light to illuminate and enliven the deep indigo purple of this space. Feel the energy flood in and cascade through the physical body.

- Breathe.

- Repeat this statement to yourself. *I speak my truth.*

- Breathe.

- Take your awareness to just below the navel center. This is the sacral chakra. The color is a rich orange. See the pelvic area as a golden bowl filled with the vibrant orange waters of creativity. You sit in the middle on a giant lotus leaf, perfectly balanced, fully supported.

- Breathe.

- No matter which way you choose to move, the liquid always returns to balance with you perfectly supported in the middle.

- Breathe.

- Repeat this statement to yourself. *I am gifted grace and harmony when I speak my truth.*

- Breathe.

- Take your awareness to the chest center. This is the heart chakra—the middle chakra, that which bridges the upper three and lower three. The color is vibrant emerald or forest green. See yourself in the middle on a vibrant pink and white lotus flower atop a green lotus leaf. You are seated in your heart, the center of unconditional love.

- Breathe.

- See the heart center flooded with Divine energy from above as life-force energy rises to meet it from below. You are supported in Love from above and below.

- Repeat this statement to yourself. *I am my own true north.*

- Breathe.

- This powerful energy from your heart center floods down your arms and out through your hands to touch the world. You are fully supported and in your power as you choose to act from your heart.

- Repeat the full affirmation, feeling Spirit, or your innate Divinity, Higher Self, or beautiful Inner Being speaking to you. *Speak your own truth; you are gifted grace and harmony when you speak your truth. You are your own true north. You are energy being human.*

- Breathe. Remain in this space, feeling this space, for as long as it feels comfortable, or as long as your schedule allows.

- When you are ready, take a deep breath and bring your awareness back to the crown.

- See the petals of the lotus closing once again—
  yours to open at will, and close at will.

- Take another long, slow breath.

- Bring your awareness back into the body. Wiggle your toes and
  fingers, gently move your hands and your head, and open your
  eyes to bring your awareness fully back into this moment.

- Express gratitude for All That Is and the gift of grace ... and
  be aware that your Source is even more grateful for all that
  you are, and all that you are becoming. And so It is.

Meditation to Connect with Archangel Jophiel, Higher Self, and Spirit Guides and Teachers

This simple meditation is often favored by those who already enjoy working
with archangels, Spirit, guides, or teachers, but please remember that they are
all aspects of our innate Divinity or essence. Whether you wish to connect
with the energy of Archangel Jophiel for support, strength, and a sense of true
beauty, or whether you wish to connect to your own Inner Being, the synergy
of the aquamarine combination will powerfully support your heartfelt intention to be present in the moment and to be open to allow that which is there
for you to flow to you.

- Please sit in your comfortable meditation position.

- Place four drops of your combined Star of Bethlehem and
  Slender Rice Flower flower essences and aquamarine crystal
  essence under the tongue, anoint your aquamarine with a drop
  of lemongrass essential oil, inhale a few drops of the expansive
  and inspiring lemongrass from a tissue or handkerchief and
  throughout the meditation if you feel inspired to do so, and
  hold your stone in lightly cupped hands.

- Settle into the position, close your eyes, and take a long, slow, deep breath, releasing any tension on the exhale. Repeat with two more breaths.

- Feeling relaxed, still, and present to the moment, please state your intentions. *I am present for all that is here for me. I am listening, and you are welcome.*

- Breathe and release any tension with a long exhalation.

- The soft sound of the breath mirrors the tranquil space of silence where inner peace and harmony are found. Feel the breath, hear the breath, and allow for any awareness of connection that follows.

- Feel deep appreciation and gratitude for this time of connection to a Divine messenger, teacher, or aspect of Oneness, and come out of the meditation whenever you are ready.

Please know that no matter what you feel or do not feel during the meditation, any question you have asked has been answered, any clarity you are seeking has been forthcoming, and any connection you desired has been facilitated by the synergy of the high vibrational combination of aquamarine crystal, lemongrass essential oil, and the aquamarine, Star of Bethlehem, and Slender Rice Flower essence blend, and Archangel Jophiel. Your conscious awareness and ability to speak your truth with grace, embrace a sense of harmony, and be your own true north have been awakened and strengthened. If this is not a familiar practice for you, please be reassured that enhanced connection is always facilitated and clarity and answers always provided. Sometimes guidance will flow into your consciousness during the practice, sometimes you will be inspired to pick up a particular book, or turn onto a certain radio or television channel, or bump into someone as you go about your day. The answers and clarity always flow, but we do not always get to micromanage how they come to us. Indeed, trusting in our inherent guidance will always deliver that which we seek in the quickest, most direct, and life-enhancing way ... we just need to trust.

Remember, it is in the smallest of moments that miracles happen and the beauty, grace, and voice of Jophiel and associated teachers and guides, including your Higher Self, facilitated through the synergy of the aquamarine combination is indeed inspired.

Aventurine, Green

TRADITIONAL CHAKRA ASSOCIATION
Heart (4th)

MAIN APPLICATIONS
Seeing Clearly • Insight • Protection
Choosing from the Heart

SYNERGISTIC COMBINATION
Crystal: Green Aventurine
Essential Oil: Bergamot
Flower Essences: Crab Apple and Philotheca
Archangel: Chamuel

The beautiful, soft green of green aventurine resonates with the heart chakra. It is the stone of chance, opportunity, and good fortune—they say one should never buy a lottery ticket or play any game of chance without green aventurine in the left pocket. This stone encourages abundance and prosperity to flow, and can open us to the pure joy of unlimited possibilities.

Green aventurine is also a great healer and a wonderful stone for healing the heart, giving support and comfort—it particularly provides soothing comfort and strength when we choose to allow the heart to reopen after a period of being shut down. It has strong healing energy for the body, mind, and spirit and balances erratic emotions, enhances perception, strengthens creative insight, encourages decisiveness, and promotes empathy and compassion.

Green aventurine is wonderful for inspiring our creativity while promoting wellness and well-being in the physical, mental, emotional, and spiritual bodies; it supports our release of blocked energy in the aura that has become stagnant, preventing or inhibiting flow. Choosing to release entrenched negative belief patterns is powerfully supported.

This stone is also highly protective in this process of release—as we become more open, and release and clear fears and negativity in all their forms, this stone protects us from others who may wish to hook into our energy in any way that would not serve us well.

We invite in clarity and awareness and become able to live through our heart space, loving all in all their imperfections. We love and accept ourselves; we are all perfect in our imperfections. We recognize the mirroring present in every interaction, giving us the opportunity to release and allow that energy to be dissolved. Our perception and intellect are therefore increased through self-examination, reflection, and self-responsibility.

How Green Aventurine Facilitates Well-Being

- This stone is a powerful comforter—its soothing energy can comfort and strengthen the heart that is daring to reopen after being shut down.

- Green aventurine can be especially supportive for those who are choosing to release inhibiting or limiting negative behavior patterns.

- It can open us to the pure joy of unlimited possibilities and the pure potentiality in each moment—aventurine was used in ancient Tibet to improve perception and creative insight (as well as helping to ease nearsightedness).

- This stone calms and balances troubled emotions, relieves stress, and stabilizes the mind, therefore speeding healing of emotional, mental, and physical bodies—our inherent male and female energies, yin and yang, are restored to balance.

- Green aventurine balances and stabilizes energy: highly useful with teenagers.

- Green aventurine offers such powerful support: it allows us to be open, soft, and adaptable without feeling too vulnerable or exposed. We become more independent, self-sustained, and capable of original thought.

. . . .

The green aventurine stone has been the crystallizing component that was the catalyst for all other components to come together, not only through resonance, but in a life-enhancing way. My beautiful palm stone often sits reassuringly in my jeans pocket, and rubbing my thumb slowly across its face is instantly recognizable to me.

Learning, accepting, and truly appreciating that none of us could be where we are today without what has been, that we are the totality of all of our experiences, is so personally liberating and empowering, and allows for compassion and understanding of others. I have been able to let go and accept the inherent gifts in every moment along the way that have made me strong—a gentle warrior who will stand and deliver when required but can equally walk away and let be what is.

One recent moment with the green aventurine synergistic combination occurred during a weekend house visit with a lifelong friend and their new partner. The visit appeared to be going well, but there was underlying tension that, to this day, has remained a mystery to me.

A few slighting remarks on top of the undercurrent left me feeling more than a little vulnerable and unsure of myself. To engage would have been inappropriate and certainly have served no good purpose, and engaging to "win" could have been damaging to all. Wisdom is knowing when to walk away. I found myself walking to the balcony.

I stood there looking but not seeing the view, and gently rubbed the synergistically prepared green aventurine in my pocket, and took a breath to connect. I do not know how long I held that trance, and it was obviously not as long in real time as it felt for me held in a place outside of time. I was able to let go of the negative feeling; I returned to the group feeling empowered and protected, and incredibly quiet and serene; the calm and peace remained with me for the weekend. Letting go is the greatest gift we give to ourselves. Forgiveness requires absolutely nothing and is quietly empowering and strengthening.

Essential Oils, Flower Essences, and Spirit Connection

Green aventurine has been embraced across time and cultures to heal and empower, but the potentialities and possibilities that it can open for us are transformed when it is used in combination. When we choose to immerse ourselves in the synergy of the following combinations, we gift ourselves an appreciation of the wonder of life.

Essential Oils

The highest resonance is between green aventurine and bergamot essential oil. Although traditionally used with the heart chakra, this power combination works effectively and synergistically to harmonize the whole being whether the crystal is placed on the body, held, worn, carried in the pocket, or placed nearby.

Bergamot (*Citrus bergamia*) oil is expressed from the peel of the citrus fruit of the evergreen tree discovered in Calabria, southern Italy, in the seventeenth century. The distinctive citrus aroma is sweet, fresh, and light, and the essence was first produced and sold in Bergamo in Italy—not to be confused with an

American native plant that is also sometimes known as bergamot (or Oswego tea) because its leaves have a similar fragrance to the true bergamot.

The pale greenish-yellow oil was one of the principal ingredients in the original Eau de Cologne (together with lemon, lavender, neroli, and rosemary), which was introduced to Europe in the early eighteenth century by an Italian living in Cologne. Bergamot also gives the popular Earl Grey tea its distinctive aroma and flavor.

Bergamot is purifying, calming, and balancing to the hypothalamus gland, the wellspring of many of our deeper fear-based emotions. The pituitary gland may be regarded as the "master gland," but it has a master: the hypothalamus. It links the nervous and endocrine systems, and controls and regulates many vital functions; and, together with the limbic system in the back brain, the hypothalamus regulates our emotional and behavioral patterns. Bergamot helps restore balance to the hypothalamus.

Psychologically, this refreshing, calming, and uplifting oil will cleanse and settle agitation, anger, and irritability, and cleanse and detoxify the negativity of jealousy; calm and support mood swings, restlessness, and panic; support feelings of loss and grief; and revitalize, refresh, and uplift when we feel depressed, despondent, discouraged, and fearful.

On the emotional barometer, bergamot particularly aligns with the emotional body transforming the negative feelings of saddened and discouraged into inspired and encouraged. Inhaling bergamot encourages us to explore the shadows within: we feel supported in our exploration, knowing that the shadows can be our greatest teachers; we come to appreciate that when we look into the shadows, we are also able to see whatever we choose to see, and however we choose to see it; we bring light to the darkness and the shadows are transformed and fade, leaving traces that support us as we move forward.

Flower Essences

The highest resonance is between green aventurine and Crab Apple Bach Flower and Philotheca Australian Bush Flower Essences.

Crab Apple is one of the Bach Flower Essences for despondency or despair; it is known as the "cleansing" remedy. Crab Apple is the remedy for despair, shame, self-disgust, and self-hatred: the Crab Apple person holds an expectation that their world and those in it should be flawless—they require order, purity, and perfection and cannot perceive it. Perceived lack of perfection deeply saddens and can grow into despair and self-disgust. Crab Apple is often used to treat conditions such as anorexia nervosa and skin complaints, reflective of emotional indicators such as problems with self-image, self-condemnation, guilt, and self-worth.

The potential Crab Apple transformation is one who is generous of spirit, untroubled, and accepting; we have clarity and wisdom to see the big picture and life from broader perspective. There is awareness that physical disorder has flowed from mental and emotional disharmony, and acceptance that we have the power to transform and transmute disharmony into harmony. We are in control of us; we get to choose; we embrace self-responsibility; we see the perfection in all our imperfections.

I am always mindful in a clinical situation that Crab Apple can take a scrubbing brush through the bowels of the unconscious and so the preparedness of a client to deal with issues is always considered. However, as a component of the green aventurine synergistic combination, its powerful cleansing is so balanced and supported that the transformation is a wonder to behold and to experience.

Philotheca is the Australian Bush Flower Essence for those who have difficulty accepting acknowledgement or praise; we feel undeserving of it, unworthy. In the negative Philotheca state, we are generous with others, giving to others that which we do not give to ourselves. We freely acknowledge and praise others but have great difficulty accepting any compliment; we are excellent listeners, but feel sharing our thoughts, feelings, hopes, and dreams with another would be an imposition.

Philotheca types are often shy about plans and successes and hide their light under a bushel, as it were. Some cultures are particularly prone to the negative practice of cutting tall poppies down to size—rather than seeing high achievers as an inspiration to be emulated, there is often suspicion of their success and a desire to bring them down. This tendency plays into the negative Philotheca state and is particularly limiting with the young who find comfort in mediocrity rather than daring to be all that they wish to be. It is very sad to see one who believes that being average is preferable to the success of being all that they could be, all that they are.

The potential positive Philotheca outcome is the inner sense of worth that enables us to receive love and acknowledgement with gratitude and appreciation of the innate perfection in all of us. We choose to allow the free-flow of positive energy into our being and so we allow love in. No longer concerned about the negativity of others, we are now able to embrace all that we are, stand in our authenticity, and selectively share our plans and successes with those ready to support us.

Archangels

The highest resonance is between green aventurine and Archangel Chamuel.

Archangel Chamuel's name has been translated as *he who sees God* and *he who seeks God*. For me, Chamuel helps the seeker see that which they seek, and the innate perfection in it all. His all-knowing sight sees the interconnectedness between physical and non-physical, which helps us see the inherent connection in all—such insight calms our Inner Being and gifts us deep inner peace. Chamuel's energy is immediate and extremely kind and loving, and cascades through the body as fluttering tingles that I find intensely reassuring.

As a powerful protector against fear and negative energies, Chamuel brings great peace, comfort, and support; strengthens our innate intuition; and encourages a view from broader perspective. Chamuel helps us find what we are looking for, materially and spiritually, and offers strong guidance to smooth the way so that we can successfully find and embrace our life purpose.

There is great freedom and inner peace to be had with the fresh insight, support, and protection from Chamuel—we see ourselves and our world with clarity; we are supported as we grow from life experience and integrate that which we know; we are motivated and encouraged to accept self-responsibility and to spread our wings and fly. We feel protected and strong, insightful and motivated, and choose to see situations from a broader perspective and to act with respect, kindness, and compassion for all concerned. There is great strength in the gentle warrior, empowered by discernment and discrimination.

. . . .

For me, there is great inner strength, peace, and freedom in the synergy of the green aventurine combination. There is a sense of powerlessness that comes when I feel a need to defend and justify my beliefs, feelings, thoughts, dreams, and aspirations—it can be very limiting. I have come to know that yielding, withholding, or walking away has nothing to do with a lack of power. The warrior fights bravely for their cause, but chooses when to engage and knows when to walk away. Yielding is not backing down; it is not giving in. Yielding is taking into account all who will be hurt (including oneself) by the fallout of continuing. It is very self-empowering!

Meditation Practices

By choosing to quiet the mind with the green aventurine synergistic combination we see with clarity and feel the power and protection of our heart space as the physical integrates with the spiritual, through the mental and emotional bodies. We embrace a sense of wonder at the innate order, balance, and perfection in it all. The infinite field of possibilities and potentialities is there for each of us. There is an elusive richness to a life that is regularly refreshed and aligned by quiet time alone in contemplation.

For the following meditations, please have at hand your crystal, essential oil, and crystal and flower essences. The crystal essence and combined flower essences may be taken in a single blend, or used separately, as is most convenient to you. The essential oil may certainly be vaporized in an oil burner to fill the meditation space, but as this is not always doable or convenient in some locations, please be assured that a few drops of essential oil on a tissue or handkerchief will serve you well at any time and in any location—whether meditating at home or in the garden, or simply connecting in while waiting for a moment to pass.

Sit in whatever way is comfortable for you—if seated in a chair, have your feet flat on the floor with no shoes. Ensure your back is straight by gently lifting your heart center. Relax your shoulders. Lengthen the back of the neck by slightly tilting the chin downward.

Take a couple of breaths and bring yourself to a place of quiet appreciation of this time that you are gifting you.

Meditation to Connect with the Green Aventurine Synergy

I regard this meditation to be the simplest and "earthiest" of the three connecting to this combination's synergy. This meditation connects us to the high vibrational energy that is created by the specific combination of these gifts from Mother Earth: green aventurine stone, bergamot essential oil, and a blend of green aventurine, Crab Apple, and Philotheca essences. As always, it is all about the synergy of the combination. I use this meditation whenever I feel in need of support, clarity, and insight that inevitably follow as I feel protected and strengthened by deep inner calm. To connect with the green aventurine synergy, you will need:

Green aventurine crystal

Bergamot essential oil

Crab Apple and Philotheca flower essences

Green aventurine crystal essence

- Place four drops of the combined Crab Apple and Philotheca flower essences and green aventurine crystal essence under your tongue. Take a breath.

- Anoint the green aventurine with a drop of bergamot essential oil. Inhale the uplifting and calming citrus aroma as you gently rub the oil into the stone, breathing slowly and deeply.

- Cup the green aventurine lightly in your hands—the fingertips of the right hand gently touch the base of the left palm—and rest your hands comfortably in your lap. Take a deep breath, softly close your eyes, and release any tension with the exhalation.

- Feel the energy of the green aventurine as it fills your cupped hands—for example, it may feel tingling, effervescent, light, heavy, or like your hands are suctioned together or they may expand apart during the session—there is no right way it should feel, and how it feels is right for you.

- Feel or imagine the energy moving up through your arms, through to your beautiful heart center, and radiating out to fill your being in whatever way feels right for you.

- Know that the synergy of the combination will calm, heal, open, or enhance that which needs attention at this time.

- You may see the soft green of the aventurine behind the closed eyes—maybe flashes, maybe an expansive sea of color, or color that fades in and out, as the energy of the green aventurine combination connects with, opens, and expands the various energy centers.

- You are safe in this space. Feel gratitude for any insights that may come to you and let them go. Trust that any clarity has settled into your being and will be with you, guiding you and protecting you when you come out of the meditation.

- Feel the energy. Be in wonder of the synergy of these combined gifts from Mother Earth. Luxuriate in the support and clarity of connection; allow it to fill you, nourish you, and sustain you. Remain within that expansive grounded space for as long as you wish.

Meditation on the Essence of the Green Aventurine Combination (with Affirmations)

This, for me, is the most powerful of the three green aventurine meditations for supporting change and empowering a heartfelt choice to lovingly and willingly let go of fears that limit us. We feel protected to view from a new perspective. Again, it is all about the synergy of the combination that lifts the vibration of our physical, emotional, mental, and spiritual bodies, and the specific affirmations are an integral component of the synergy of this meditation practice. The affirmations allow and facilitate change in ways that continually surprise and delight me—the words remain unchanged each time, but the results are as different as I am each time I change and grow, and then return to this inspired affirmation practice using the green aventurine combination.

- Please sit in your comfortable meditation position.

- Place four drops of your combined Crab Apple and Philotheca flower essences and green aventurine crystal essence under the tongue, anoint your green aventurine with a drop of bergamot essential oil and inhale a few drops of bergamot from a tissue or handkerchief while holding your stone in lightly cupped hands.

- Settle into the position, close your eyes, and take a long, slow, deep breath, releasing any tension on the exhale. Repeat with two more breaths.

- Take your awareness behind the eyebrow center. This is the third eye chakra. The color is deep indigo or purple. See yourself sitting in the middle of this space—the one in the middle who intuitively knows.

- Breathe.

- Take your awareness to the crown above you. See it layered with the petals of a closed lotus flower and imagine those petals unfolding, opening to pure positive energy and the infinite field of possibilities.

- Allow the pure white light to illuminate and enliven the deep indigo purple of this space. Feel the energy flood in and cascade through the physical body.

- Breathe.

- Repeat this statement to yourself. *I can see clearly now.*

- Breathe.

- Take your awareness to just below the navel center. This is the sacral chakra. The color is a rich orange. See the pelvic area as a golden bowl filled with the vibrant orange waters of creativity. You sit in the middle on a giant lotus leaf, perfectly balanced, fully supported.

- Breathe.

- No matter which way you choose to move, the liquid always returns to balance with you perfectly supported in the middle.

- Breathe.

- Repeat this statement to yourself. *I am powerfully protected.*

- Breathe.

- Take your awareness to the chest center. This is the heart chakra—the middle chakra, that which bridges the upper three and lower three. The color is vibrant emerald or forest green. See yourself in the middle on a vibrant pink and white lotus flower atop a green lotus leaf. You are seated in your heart, the center of unconditional love.

- Breathe.

- See the heart center flooded with Divine energy from above as life-force energy rises to meet it from below. You are supported in Love from above and below.

- Repeat this statement to yourself. *I am safe to choose from the heart.*

- Breathe.

- This powerful energy from your heart center floods down your arms and out through your hands to touch the world. You are fully supported and in your power as you choose to act from your heart.

- Repeat the full affirmation, feeling Spirit, or your innate Divinity, Higher Self, or beautiful Inner Being speaking to you. *You see clearly now. There is innate perfection and you feel powerfully protected. You are safe and powerful when you choose from the heart. You are energy being human.*

- Breathe. Remain in this space, feeling this space, for as long as it feels comfortable, or as long as your schedule allows.

- When you are ready, take a deep breath and bring your awareness back to the crown. See the petals of the lotus flower closing once again—yours to open at will, and close at will.

- Take another long, slow breath.

- Bring your awareness back into the body. Wiggle your toes and fingers, gently move your hands and your head, and open your eyes to bring your awareness fully back into this moment.

- Express gratitude for All That Is and the gift of grace ... and be aware that your Source is even more grateful for all that you are, and all that you are becoming. And so It is.

Meditation to Connect with Archangel Chamuel, Higher Self, and Spirit Guides and Teachers

This simple meditation is often favored by those who already enjoy working with archangels, Spirit, guides, or teachers, but please remember that they are all aspects of our innate Divinity or essence. Whether you wish to connect with the energy of Archangel Chamuel for strength, peace, insight, and clarity, or whether you wish to connect to your own Inner Being, the synergy of the green aventurine combination will powerfully support your heartfelt intention to be present in the moment and to be open to allow that which is there for you to flow to you.

- Please sit in your comfortable meditation position.

- Place four drops of your combined Crab Apple and Philotheca flower essences and green aventurine crystal essence under the tongue, anoint your green aventurine with a drop of bergamot essential oil, inhale a few drops of the inspirational encouragement of bergamot oil from a tissue or handkerchief and throughout the meditation if you feel inspired to do so, and hold your stone in lightly cupped hands.

- Settle into the position, close your eyes, and take a long, slow, deep breath, releasing any tension on the exhale. Repeat with two more breaths.

- Feeling relaxed, still, and present to the moment, please state your intentions. *I am present for all that is here for me. I am listening, and you are welcome.*

- Breathe and release any tension with a long exhalation.

- The soft sound of the breath mirrors the tranquil space of silence where inner peace and harmony are found. Feel the breath, hear the breath, and allow for any awareness of connection that follows.

- Feel deep appreciation and gratitude for this time of connection to a Divine messenger, teacher, or aspect of Oneness, and come out of the meditation whenever you are ready.

Please know that no matter what you feel or do not feel during the meditation, any question you have asked has been answered, any clarity you are seeking has been forthcoming, and any connection you desired has been facilitated by the synergy of the high vibrational combination of green aventurine crystal, bergamot essential oil, and the green aventurine, Crab Apple, and Philotheca essence blend, and Archangel Chamuel. Your conscious awareness and ability to see situations more clearly with heightened insight, and to feel protected and safe to choose from your powerful heart have been awakened and strengthened. If this is not a familiar practice for you, please be reassured that enhanced connection is always facilitated and clarity and answers always provided. Sometimes guidance will flow into your consciousness during the practice, sometimes you will be inspired to pick up a particular book, or turn onto a certain radio or television channel, or bump into someone as you go about your day. The answers and clarity always flow, but we do not always get to micromanage how they come to us. Indeed, trusting in our inherent guidance will always deliver that which we seek in the quickest, most direct, and life-enhancing way ... we just need to trust.

Remember, it is in the smallest of moments that miracles happen and the clarity and powerful protection of Chamuel and associated teachers and guides, including your Higher Self, facilitated through the synergy of the green aventurine combination is indeed inspired.

Carnelian

TRADITIONAL CHAKRA ASSOCIATION
Sacral (2nd)

MAIN APPLICATIONS
Inner Strength • Innate Perfection and Balance
Self-Empowerment • Shining Brightly

SYNERGISTIC COMBINATION
Crystal: Carnelian
Essential Oil: Ylang-ylang
Flower Essences: Scleranthus and Southern Cross
Archangel: Uriel

Carnelian is a form of quartz that in times past was considered strictly for the ruling class, and those of high social status were buried with carnelian to protect them on their journey.

Carnelian resonates with the sacral chakra, Swadhisthana in yogic traditions—the deep orange stone beautifully bridges the red of the base chakra below and the yellow of the solar plexus chakra above. The sacral chakra relates to our sense of creativity, sensuality, balance, and our emotions; this area also relates to the Hara in traditional Japanese Reiki and the Zen Knowing Mind. It is a stone that has become a constant for me.

Balancing the sacral chakra balances our emotions, and similarly, carnelian stabilizes and anchors us in the now, leaving that which has passed. Carnelian protects and heals at a deep emotional level. It encourages acceptance of the cycles of life—everything passes, and this too shall pass.

This wonderful stone is a powerful energy booster. For those needing more pep in life, it will boost vitality and increase energy flow to us and through us. Carnelian attracts and gives energy, protects against negative vibrations, enhances a sense of humor, and calms tempers. Powerful carnelian cleanses and clears other stones.

Carnelian helps overcome insecurity by reinforcing our inherent strength within and encouraging positive choices so that we can step into our power. It is a stone of optimism and creativity, stimulating positive action, and deepening a trust in one's own ability to manifest and create in this world. Carnelian helps us embrace our creative energy and overcome the fear of failure or fear of making a wrong decision that so often paralyze us in non-action—we are taken out of analysis paralysis into daring to choose and decide, and embrace change and transformation, with quiet assuredness and optimism.

Negative life experiences and energy may be recycled, and if one chooses, released and dissolved to be transmuted into pure positive energy for redistribution for the highest good.

Carnelian is very helpful for those who have suffered any type of abuse and can illuminate the path back to our innate self-empowerment when self-esteem and self-worth have been trampled.

How Carnelian Facilitates Well-Being

- Carnelian offers powerful protection—emotionally, it
  protects against anger, rage, envy, and resentment (ours
  and that of others). In addition, anger is calmed and
  negative emotional energies are replaced with a love of life.

- It supports deep emotional healing and overcoming abuse, strengthening our sense of self-empowerment.

- It brings courage to make life-enhancing choices, dissolves apathy, dispels self-doubt, and motivates us to move forward.

- In meditation it can help remove unwanted thoughts, vibrationally aligning daydreams and visualizations to facilitate the physical experience of them.

- We learn to trust our inner guidance, intuition, and gut feelings and speak our truth with a sense and intent of peace and harmony.

- Carnelian enhances how and what we think by improving analytical ability and clarifying perception. Concentration is sharpened, mental lethargy is dispelled, and analysis paralysis is released.

....

The synergy of the carnelian combination has particularly resonated with me, and supported, stimulated, and stabilized me along my path of curiosity. When I was exploring the use of gifts from the Earth to enhance our connection with All That Is, there was a synergistic connection that lacked clarity. I decided to surrender to the confusion and just let it be, and to see it simply as an opportunity to exercise trust in the process that I had chosen to embrace—there was no need for me to control it. However, impatience can soon lead me into self-doubt, so I chose to use the carnelian synergistic combination to support me, popped the prepared stone into a cage pendant, and chose to trust that I was not failing in my quest. I would let it go and all would unfold perfectly.

The following week I received free tickets to a weekend body and soul fair, and then felt intuitively drawn to visit a particular stand number—the stand was a crystal seller. The only stone that I felt drawn to and picked up was unlabeled and unfamiliar to me. It looked dullish and decidedly unloved, so I asked the seller to identify the stone. The choice was purely intuitive and inspired. It was the very stone for the synergistic combination around which I'd previously felt confusion—my intention to let go and not micromanage the process had been powerfully supported and guided by the synergy of the carnelian combination. Synchronicity!

I purchased the stone, felt an instant powerful and clear resonance with one particular essential oil and cleared and programmed the crystal to guide me to connection for the highest good. However, the usual powerful resonance with the other components eluded me. I continually returned to my beloved carnelian stone and synergistic combination for inspiration and chose to not worry over this other elusive combination, as had been my tendency in the past—I could be intensely focused and wear myself out worrying over endless alternatives when I could not quite find an answer. Interestingly, beautiful cascading tingles of connection followed each time I gently cupped the caged carnelian at my heart center, and returned the new crystal to the shelf, as if being reassured that all was well, but this was not the time to work with this new crystal. The whole experience was such a wonderfully practical exercise in trusting the innate perfection in each unfolding!

My search for the new synergistic combination was completed in time, but my heart pounds with the memory of this wonderful unfolding—just one of the life-enhancing moments facilitated by this carnelian synergistic combination, for which I am grateful.

Each component of the carnelian synergistic combination brings powerful possibilities and, after reviewing the contribution of each, I'm sure you will appreciate the synergy. The carnelian combination facilitates and supports self-empowerment, self-responsibility, and self-determination, as we clearly see each of life's moments as a creation, a nudge from our Higher Self, to trust in the unfolding, see the inherent opportunities, and return to our innate life-enhancing and life-sustaining balance.

Essential Oils, Flower Essences, and Spirit Connection

Carnelian is a powerful stone, of that there is no doubt—the ruling classes chose wisely in times past. However, to combine the brilliance of carnelian with the following gifts is to unleash the synergy that transforms and empowers in ways that will surprise and delight, and encourage you to shine brightly.

Essential Oils

The highest resonance is between carnelian and ylang-ylang essential oil. Traditionally, carnelian is used with the sacral chakra but this power combination works effectively and synergistically to harmonize the whole being whether placed on the body, held, worn, carried in the pocket, or placed nearby.

Ylang-ylang (*Cananga odorata*) is distilled from the flowers of the ylang-ylang tree. Native to South East Asia, in particular Indonesia and the Philippines, it is known as the perfume tree, and the name means *flower of flowers* because of its exotic aroma. The flowers are handpicked at dawn, and if bruised will spoil quickly and blacken.

The heady aroma of ylang-ylang is sweet, sensual, and exotic. It is relaxing, calming, and uplifting, and supports reconnection with our emotions to help relieve all manifestations of disharmony and unbalance, including anger, agitation, anxiety, frustration, nervous tension, irritability, depression, moodiness, lack of self-worth, and so much more. It promotes restful sleep when struggling with insomnia or nightmares, and can be an amazing aid for relieving fears that so often stifle us from acting on our passion.

On the emotional barometer, ylang-ylang balances the emotions to shift from angry and volatile into mindfulness and calm. The intense aroma helps us break old entrenched habits and negative patterns, encouraging flexibility that comes from acceptance of the myriad contrasts and possibilities open to us in every situation.

Retaining anger deep inside negatively impacts us mentally, emotionally, and physically—stored anger damages the body on a cellular level; our bodies become acidic, our tissues become toxic, and our immune systems struggle. Mentally, emotionally, and spiritually, we become closed to all of the possibilities and potentialities open to us. We become locked in struggle and blinded to our innate inner resources, making concentration and attention impossible, while decision-making becomes clouded and strained as we lack any sense of mental clarity or self-potential.

Everything in the universe is in constant motion—movement is integral to all life and matter. Emotion is energy (E) in motion, and once our emotions become stuck, then we are negatively impacted on every level. Emotion becomes energy *demanding motion*, rather than *in motion*.

Ylang-ylang strikes at the heart of the inner storm that holds us in our negative patterning, releasing our emotions to flow and restore natural balance. Our magnificent bodies continually seek homeostasis, or balance, on every level and the combination of exotic ylang-ylang with vibrant carnelian enhances restoration and maintenance of our innate perfection.

Flower Essences

The highest resonance is between carnelian and Scleranthus Bach Flower and Southern Cross Australian Bush Flower Essences.

Scleranthus is the Bach Flower Essence for when we feel unbalanced by choices available to us and therefore become stuck in indecision or hesitation. There is uncertainty as we may endlessly vacillate between this way or that way, and feel very unsure whichever way we choose would be the best. Furthermore, our moods seem to toss us from one extreme to the other. Instead of seeing a situation to be a defining moment in life, we slip back into letting the moment define us—the choice is always ours. Like Alice in Wonderland, we come to the fork in the road and cannot decide which way, and get stuck at the crossroads—but as the Cheshire Cat points out, if we do not know where we wish to go, then it matters not which road we take—defining the moment may be as simple as embracing the adventure of choosing to try a new path.

We may suffer the grasshopper mind, hopping from one thought to another, or the magpie mind full of useless bits and pieces, and confuse or annoy friends and family with our erratic conversations. We also might habitually run late through our dithering or go through the debilitating cycle of publicly being "up," appearing to be clear and decisive only to suffer the private "down" of doubting and regretting all that we've said and done. Indecision and self-doubt can be crippling and debilitating to body and spirit.

The potential Scleranthus transformation fills us with calm determination and a quiet ability to remain poised and balanced at each turn. We feel mentally clear, sharp, quick to analyze, and able to assess, discriminate, and decide. Our calm assuredness, balance, poise, and grace fill our whole being, which is empowering to us and soothing to others. As we find our innate inner rhythm, we feel supported, attuned, and perfectly balanced, which allows us to offer others compassion and understanding as we gift them our complete attention.

Southern Cross is the Australian Bush Flower Essence for when we have a sense of lack in our life. We complain and feel bitter (often silently) about the hand we've been dealt, and may even feel the struggle of the martyr. We are totally out of sync, often feeling emotionally tossed around in life's washing machine, with only small pauses between the agitation of the wash cycle and the out-of-control speed of the spin cycle.

The potential Southern Cross transformation returns us to our innate balance, where we take responsibility for our own feelings of self-worth and self-respect, and stand firmly in our own personal power feeling optimistic and positive about the choices and possibilities that are open to us—we are fully aware that we create our own reality, and in every moment can create negatively or positively. We embrace a renewed compassion and gentleness for others who are in emotional struggle—we've been there.

·············

I have always been mentally strong, and I have always been highly emotional and passionate. There is always the correlating opposite in this world of duality, so I have also been prone to indecision as alternate scenarios flowed easily to me causing dithering, hesitation, and worry for fear of getting it wrong. I have also been prone to deep hurt emotionally, unable to easily shrug off or let go of the pain.

It's not rocket science to see why this carnelian synergistic combination resonated with me so powerfully when I first began testing these combinations for resonance and why I still enjoy the support of the anointed carnelian on a daily basis, and the complete synergistic combination regularly.

Archangels

The highest resonance is between carnelian and Archangel Uriel.

Archangel Uriel is considered one of the wisest of the Archangels and his quiet guiding energy has become a mainstay in my life. He is also one of the four archangels who particularly facilitate healing: Michael, Raphael, Uriel, and Haniel. His energy flows to us quickly whenever requested and can be relied upon for intellectual clarity, answers and information, as well as practical down-to-earth solutions to a problem. It can be a multifaceted matter that requires mental acuity and attention, or a matter as simple as remembering a name as a familiar face nods from across the street. The key is that when we ask, Uriel pops the answer into our head. We enjoy the confidence of answers that just come to us.

Uriel brings light to illuminate situations and to light our path forward. He brings creative insight and strengthens our innate sense of prophecy and intuition; he brings the perfect balance of intellectual clarity, understanding and knowledge, spiritual knowing, and deep emotional healing and balance that comes from appreciation of broader perspective. He strengthens us mentally with enhanced powers of focus, attention, and concentration, while he strengthens us creatively by sparking ideas and solutions that are both practical and inspired.

Apart from bringing mystical predictions and sacred geometry to humans, Archangel Uriel is also traditionally known as the one who originally brought knowledge of alchemy to the physical realm, that mysterious process of turning base metal into precious gold that has since eluded alchemists down through the ages. My personal experience and knowledge of alchemy is through energy, and I feel no greater joy and appreciation than when facilitating the transformation of negative energy into pure positive energy. It is always a great privilege to hold the space for a friend or client while they willingly and lovingly release fear and negativity and then refill, recharge, and revitalize with the infinite energy of Divine Love that is ever-present for all of us.

Uriel powerfully supports, protects, guides, teaches, and inspires a life path that is connected and illuminated by the unfading light of Love and clarity. We succeed in ways we may not even have dared to dream as we embrace the guidance and balance of ease and flow and allow the natural rhythm of life to be restored.

He brings a sense of self-responsibility and self-empowerment and encourages us to feel light and supported as we confidently choose with an appreciation of broader perspective in each moment. We feel emotionally and physically restored and re-energized with vitality and Divine life-force energy.

. . . .

I am, by nature, curious and enjoy exploring and living in the wonder of Life. I now know that Uriel's energy has long supported my curiosity, either directly with answers, or by inspired action that leads me to where I will find them— the only difference is that I now use this guidance with awareness. Indeed, I am aware that often even the question is inspired, and then the answer, when it facilitates my quest at the time.

Carnelian charged with ylang-ylang essential oil is pretty much a constant in my life these days, with Archangel Uriel standing behind illuminating the way through my heart chakra and Hara (sacral chakra).

Meditation Practices

By choosing to quiet the mind with the carnelian synergistic combination we come to know that there is no failure from broader perspective—sometimes choices may not turn out as we expect, and so we learn, and simply choose again. We embrace a sense of ease and flow, trusting the innate balance and perfection in it all and feel empowered to be however we choose to be. The infinite field of possibilities and potentialities is there for each of us. There is an elusive richness to a life that is regularly refreshed and aligned by quiet time alone in contemplation.

For the following meditations, please have at hand your crystal, essential oil, and crystal and flower essences. The crystal essence and combined flower essences may be taken in a single blend, or used separately, as is most convenient to you. The essential oil may certainly be vaporized in an oil burner to fill the meditation space, but as this is not always doable or convenient in some locations, please be assured that a few drops of essential oil on a tissue or handkerchief will serve you well at any time and in any location—whether meditating at home or in the car at lunchtime, or simply connecting in when you feel bogged down and unclear.

Sit in whatever way is comfortable for you—if seated in a chair, have your feet flat on the floor with no shoes. Ensure your back is straight by gently lifting your heart center. Relax your shoulders. Lengthen the back of the neck by slightly tilting the chin downward.

Take a couple of breaths and bring yourself to a place of quiet appreciation of this time that you are gifting you.

Meditation to Connect with the Carnelian Synergy

This is perhaps the easiest and "earthiest" of the three meditations. In this carnelian meditation, we connect to the high vibrational energy that is created by the specific combination of these gifts from Mother Earth: carnelian stone, ylang-ylang essential oil, and a blend of carnelian, Scleranthus, and Southern Cross essences. As always, it is all about the synergy of the combination. I use this meditation whenever I feel in need of the calm assuredness, balance, and understanding that inevitably follow as I am inspired and uplifted. To connect with the carnelian synergy, you will need:

Carnelian crystal

Ylang-ylang essential oil

Scleranthus and Southern Cross flower essences

Carnelian crystal essence

- Place four drops of the combined Scleranthus and Southern Cross flower essences and carnelian crystal essence under your tongue. Take a breath.

- Anoint the deep rich orange carnelian stone with a drop of ylang-ylang essential oil. Inhale the intensely exotic aroma as you gently rub the oil into the stone, breathing slowly and deeply.

- Cup the carnelian lightly in your hands—the fingertips of the right hand gently touch the base of the left palm—and rest your hands comfortably in your lap. Take a deep breath, softly close your eyes, and release any tension with the exhalation.

- Feel the energy of the carnelian as it fills your cupped hands—for example, it may feel tingling, effervescent, light, heavy, or like your hands are suctioned together or they may expand apart during the session—there is no right way it should feel, and how it feels is right for you.

- Feel or imagine the energy moving up through your arms and through to the heart center, from where it radiates out to fill your being in whatever way feels right for you.

- Know that the synergy of the combination will balance, heal, open, or enhance that which needs attention at this time.

- You may see the deep orange of the carnelian behind the closed eyes—maybe flashes, maybe spiraling color, or color that fades in and out, as the energy of the carnelian combination connects with, balances, and expands the various energy centers.

- Feel gratitude for any clarity or inspired thoughts that may come to you and let them go. Trust that all have settled into your being and will be there for you when you come out of the meditation.

- Feel the energy. Be in wonder of the synergy of these combined gifts from Mother Earth. Luxuriate in the harmony of connection; allow it to fill you, expand, nourish, and sustain you. Remain within that expansive grounded space for as long as you wish.

Meditation on the Essence of the Carnelian Combination (with Affirmations)

Undoubtedly, of the three carnelian meditations, this one most powerfully supports a decision to change. We are reassured in our heartfelt decision to release what has been limiting us and empowered to dare to allow ourselves to shine. Again, it is all about the synergy of the combination that lifts the vibration of our physical, emotional, mental, and spiritual bodies, and the specific affirmations are an integral component of the synergy of this meditation practice. The affirmations allow and facilitate change in ways that continually surprise and delight me—the words remain unchanged each time, but the results are as different as I am each time I change and grow, and then return to this inspired carnelian affirmation practice.

- Please sit in your comfortable meditation position.

- Place four drops of your combined Scleranthus and Southern Cross flower essences and carnelian crystal essence under the tongue, anoint your carnelian with a drop of ylang-ylang essential oil and inhale a few drops of ylang-ylang from a tissue or handkerchief while holding your stone in lightly cupped hands.

- Settle into the position, close your eyes, and take a long, slow, deep breath, releasing any tension on the exhale. Repeat with two more breaths.

- Take your awareness behind the eyebrow center. This is the third eye chakra. The color is deep indigo or purple. See yourself sitting in the middle of this space—the one in the middle who intuitively knows.

- Breathe.

- Take your awareness to the crown above you. See it layered with the petals of a closed lotus flower and imagine those petals unfolding, opening to pure positive energy and the infinite field of possibilities.

- Allow the pure white light to illuminate and enliven the deep indigo purple of this space. Feel the energy flood in and cascade through the physical body.

- Breathe.

- Repeat this statement to yourself. *I cannot fail—there is no failure.*

- Breathe.

- Take your awareness to just below the navel center. This is the sacral chakra. The color is a rich orange. See the pelvic area as a golden bowl filled with the vibrant orange waters of creativity. You sit in the middle on a giant lotus leaf, perfectly balanced, fully supported.

- Breathe.

- No matter which way you choose to move, the liquid always returns to balance with you perfectly supported in the middle.

- Breathe.

- Repeat this statement to yourself. *I am gifted innate perfection and balance.*

- Breathe.

- Take your awareness to the chest center. This is the heart chakra—the middle chakra, that which bridges the upper three and lower three. The color is vibrant emerald or forest green. See yourself in the middle on a vibrant pink and white lotus flower atop a green lotus leaf. You are seated in your heart, the center of unconditional love.

- Breathe.

- See the heart center flooded with Divine energy from above as life-force energy rises to meet it from below. You are supported in Love from above and below.

- Repeat this statement to yourself. *I am however I choose to be and I shine brightly.*

- Breathe.

- This powerful energy from your heart center floods down your arms and out through your hands to touch the world. You are fully supported and in your power as you choose to act from your heart.

- Repeat the full affirmation, feeling Spirit, or your innate Divinity, Higher Self, or beautiful Inner Being speaking to you. *You cannot fail. Your perfection and balance are innate—be all that you choose to be and shine brightly. You are energy being human.*

- Breathe. Remain in this space, feeling this space, for as long as it feels comfortable, or as long as your schedule allows.

- When you are ready, take a deep breath and bring your awareness back to the crown. See the petals of the lotus flower closing once again—yours to open at will, and close at will.

- Take another long, slow breath.

- Bring your awareness back into the body. Wiggle your toes and fingers, gently move your hands and your head, and open your eyes to bring your awareness fully back into this moment.

- Express gratitude for All That Is and the gift of grace ... and be aware that your Source is even more grateful for all that you are, and all that you are becoming. And so It is.

Meditation to Connect with Archangel Uriel, Higher Self, and Spirit Guides and Teachers

This simple meditation is often favored by those who already enjoy working with archangels, Spirit, guides, or teachers, but please remember that they are all aspects of our innate Divinity or essence. Whether you wish to connect with the energy of Archangel Uriel for clarity, illumination or understanding, or whether you wish to connect to your own Inner Being, the synergy of the carnelian combination will powerfully support your heartfelt intention to be present in the moment and to be open to allow that which is there for you to flow to you.

- Please sit in your comfortable meditation position.

- If you have a question or a situation with which you would like clarity or guiding support, bring that to mind.

- If you have a favorite invocation or preferred ritual for connecting to your teachers, guides or Spirit, please use that which feels right for you.

- Place four drops of your combined Scleranthus and Southern Cross flower essences and carnelian crystal essence under the tongue, anoint your carnelian with a drop of ylang-ylang essential oil, inhale a few drops of the exotic mindfulness of ylang-ylang oil from a tissue or handkerchief and throughout the meditation if you feel inspired to do so, and hold your stone in lightly cupped hands.

- Settle into the position, close your eyes, and take a long, slow, deep breath, releasing any tension on the exhale. Repeat with two more breaths.

- Feeling relaxed, still, and present to the moment, please state your intentions. *I am present for all that is here for me. I am listening, and you are welcome.*

- Breathe and release any tension with a long exhalation.

- The soft sound of the breath mirrors the tranquil space of silence where inner peace and harmony are found. Feel the breath, hear the breath, and allow for any awareness of connection that follows.

- Feel deep appreciation and gratitude for this time of connection to a Divine messenger, teacher, or aspect of Oneness, and come out of the meditation whenever you are ready.

Please know that no matter what you feel or do not feel during the meditation, any question you have asked has been answered, any clarity you are seeking has been forthcoming, and any connection you desired has been facilitated by the synergy of the high vibrational combination of carnelian crystal, ylang-ylang essential oil, and the carnelian, Scleranthus, and Southern Cross essence blend, and Archangel Uriel. Your conscious awareness of the inner strength that flows from understanding and appreciating your innate perfection and balance, and of self-empowerment to shine brightly with your own inner light have been awakened, heightened, and illuminated for you. If this is not a familiar practice for you, please be reassured that enhanced connection is always facilitated and clarity and answers always provided. Sometimes guidance will flow into your consciousness during the practice, sometimes you will be inspired to pick up a particular book, or turn onto a certain radio or television channel, or bump into someone as you go about your day. The answers and clarity always flow, but we do not always get to micromanage how they come to us. Indeed, trusting in our inherent guidance will always deliver that which we seek in the quickest, most direct, and life-enhancing way ... we just need to trust.

Remember, it is in the smallest of moments that miracles happen and the guiding light of Uriel and associated teachers and guides, including your Higher Self, facilitated through the synergy of the carnelian combination is indeed inspired and enlightening.

Citrine

TRADITIONAL CHAKRA ASSOCIATION
Sacral (2nd) • Solar Plexus (3rd) • Crown (7th)

MAIN APPLICATIONS
Renewed Vitality • Abundance • Self-Value • Inspiration

SYNERGISTIC COMBINATION
Crystal: Citrine
Essential Oil: Sandalwood
Flower Essences: Wild Oat and Tall Yellow Top
Archangel: Jeremiel

Citrine is a golden-brownish stone—it is actually amethyst, heated and trans-formed in the crust of the Earth. In some cases, stones are often heat-treated at high temperatures emulating the process, which is why citrine attracts a degree of discussion and concern as to whether one is buying a natural stone or one that has been heat-treated. There is disagreement about whether the stone's inherent attributes have been affected. I do not share these concerns. In fact, no matter how they are created, I have found the energy of citrine stones to be quite distinct from amethyst, their applications unique, and their effectiveness all that I have anticipated.

Citrine is a dynamic stone of success, prosperity, and abundance in health, wealth, and inner happiness. Often known as the Merchant's Stone, citrine will support business prosperity and enhance the flow of money—money is, of course, just another manifestation of energy.

A powerful cleanser, detoxifier, regenerator, and motivator, citrine emulates the sun radiating power and positive energy: warming, energizing, invigorating, sustaining, and creating. Citrine absorbs, dissolves, transmutes, dissipates, and grounds negative energy. Indeed, it deals with negative energy so completely that it needs no cleaning itself. This powerful holistic healer is highly protective of the Earth and of us, on every level, as it protects, cleanses, and balances the subtle bodies with the physical, and clears any space of negative energy.

It opens us to new ideas (or old ideas, forgotten) and facilitates and strengthens self-esteem, self-belief, and self-worth. We appreciate the natural flow of our innate gifts of joy, abundance, and manifestation; we are protected from the abuse of others, which further supports our enhanced awareness of all that we have.

Citrine facilitates correction of all personal power imbalances: overassertiveness or abuse of us, or by us, and lack of assertiveness (abuse of self). Destructive, self-sabotaging tendencies are released and removed, and a mentality of lack on any level is released.

It supports a review of our beliefs to release those that do not serve us well, and facilitates a balanced use of our innate will that orients us toward inspired leadership and guidance. We happily serve others, enjoy guiding others, but do not lose ourselves along the way—service is not servitude.

Clarity of thought and awareness are promoted and enhanced, and we are able to embrace discrimination and optimism as we jump in and go with the flow rather than holding tight to a past that no longer serves us well.

How Citrine Facilitates Well-Being

- Citrine connects to Higher Self and our inner wisdom, enhancing the ability to speak our truth with a sense of self-worth and self-responsibility.

- It promotes joy and facilitates the release of negative thought patterns and fears—we overcome fear of responsibility and anger.

- This stone facilitates awareness of the natural flow, balancing our feelings and emotions.

- It relieves stress, depression, panic attacks, anxiety, fears, and phobias; strengthens focus and concentration; and enhances intuition and psychic awareness.

- Citrine encourages us to be adventurous, try new experiences and enjoy taste-testing from the smorgasbord of life—we learn to enjoy exploring new possibilities until we find that which serves us best.

. . . .

I find it a wonderfully protected unfolding when I have chosen to review and release with the support of the citrine synergistic combination; we can review and see things from a less attached perspective without the charged emotional hook and release what has been limiting us and holding us back. Obviously, each review is different as each brings to the surface more or less emotional moments, but no matter the potential intensity of the moment, we are protected and supported by the synergy of this citrine combination as we review from this different perspective.

For me, entrenched negative patterns rooted in perceived criticisms about not being good enough, and offhand consolatory remarks, were uncovered. Small moments, a passing remark that became predictable in its regularity but long since forgotten, came back into conscious memory, and it was so interesting to view them now, at this distance.

Success was routinely minimized or kept secret for fear of upsetting or distressing others—I knew how it felt to be made to continually suffer comparison and to be considered not quite as good, and so I would do whatever it took to save another feeling that way. I became the perfectionist who encouraged others and enthusiastically celebrated their every achievement—but the same rules did not apply to me: I could easily find fault with even the highest success. It is so liberating to no longer feel the limitation of competition—letting go of needing to achieve no longer allows others to judge because we just do not hear them.

Early life moments impact our choice and ability to embrace, or limit, all that we are able to be—throughout our lives. We do not need to have suffered some great injustice or some mind-numbing abuse, nor do we need to have executed some act of great shame or done something that has caused us to be laden with great guilt, to undertake a life review that is life-enhancing, freeing, and transformational. Indeed, it is in the smallest of moments that the greatest opportunity for change so often occurs—to be able to look back across my life and be truly and deeply grateful for the contribution that each and every person has made along the way brings more joy and peace than words can describe.

Essential Oils, Flower Essences, and Spirit Connection

Citrine reinvigorates and benefits our whole being exceptionally well on its own, but when used in a synergistic combination, the energy and benefits are powerfully enhanced in surprising ways. The following combinations will help facilitate transformation without limitation that feels truly wondrous.

Essential Oils

Citrine is traditionally associated with the sacral, solar plexus, and crown chakras, and lemon and sandalwood essential oils have been cited by others as resonating with citrine at the various energy centers. However, the undoubtedly highest resonance is between citrine and sandalwood essential oil. This power combination works effectively and synergistically to harmonize the whole being whether the crystal is placed on the body, held, worn, carried in the pocket, or placed nearby.

Sandalwood (*Santalum album*) species is the best sandalwood essential oil; it is distilled from the heartwood of trees grown in India, which are now owned and controlled by the Indian government to ensure species survival. The name "sandalwood" comes from the Sanskrit *chandana*, and this characteristic sweet woody aroma has been used across the ages. It remains integral to many Eastern funeral ceremonies and is used in temples and to facilitate a deeper meditation in various practices.

Australia grows another sandalwood species (*Santalum spicatum*) with very similar therapeutic properties to the traditional Indian sandalwood. West Indian sandalwood (*Schimmelia oieifera*) is actually a completely different species, yet its therapeutic qualities are similar. Generally, West Indian sandalwood is cheaper than Indian, or Mysore, sandalwood. However, all sandalwood oils are among the more expensive.

Sandalwood, which has a greenish-yellow tinge, is celebrated for its spiritual and mood-uplifting qualities, but is also calming, relaxing, and stress-reducing. It helps us to uncover suppressed emotions and to reconnect with our feelings and emotions.

Psychologically it helps release fear and its manifestations of agitation, anger, bitterness, guilt, irritability, and jealousy; it helps counter and relieve apathy, boredom, despondency, unhelpful daydreaming, discouragement, lethargy, mood swings, and sorrow; and it also helps clear confusion, forgetfulness and poor concentration. We are revitalized, motivated, optimistic, and focused.

On the emotional barometer, there is a connection to the spiritual body where entrenched negative emotions or lifestyle choices are released by the innate life-enhancing desire to be still and reflective. This warm, mellow spicy fragrance facilitates a view from broader perspective—we take time to just be; we connect with that which we are; we see that which we are; we feel strong and protected, motivated and uplifted; we choose anew with clarity and insight that comes from reflection and review.

Flower Essences

The highest resonance is between citrine and Wild Oat Bach Flower and Tall Yellow Top Australian Bush Flower Essences.

Wild Oat is another Bach Flower Essence for uncertainty, but unlike the Scleranthus indecision between clear choices that we previously discussed as part of the carnelian synergistic combination, the Wild Oat remedy picture is for those who simply cannot identify their purpose or what they should be doing, what is right for them. They are often very talented, even multitalented, and ambitious to do well and make a difference, but feel despondent and unfulfilled because they cannot find their intended life path. They might feel they have something special to offer, but have no idea what that might be; they may float from group to group seeking intellectual or spiritual connection only to push the group away with self-sabotaging harsh judgments, or walk away themselves feeling empty and frustrated.

The Wild Oat person is searching for direction and connection with "something," unaware that they need only go within; they need only reconnect with that which sits in the middle at the core of each of us and knows—our inner guidance and Higher Self.

They may also hold entrenched negative patterns or core beliefs that go back to formative years, or go back over a lifetime, and now tend to self-sabotage by jumping from skill to skill—jack of all trades and master of none, never staying long enough at anything, never allowing others to get too close for fear inadequacies are disclosed, and therefore depriving themselves of a sense of achievement and self-worth.

The potential Wild Oat transformation brings a sense of purpose to life, and that deep happiness that comes from a clearly defined path and talents developed to their full potential. There is great inner joy when one finds their life purpose is to master and share their many skills and talents for the benefit of all concerned.

Tall Yellow Top is the Australian Bush Flower Essence for those who feel a lack of connection with those around them and/or what they are doing; they may feel isolated and even alienated; there is a sense of aloneness, if not loneliness.

As the name implies, Tall Yellow Top is a sunny yellow flower, like the golden citrine stone, and the Tall Yellow Top person often has a disconnect between the heart and the head—any decisions, choices, or responses come from the head, not from their heart as they are not in touch with their feelings. This learned response may have become entrenched over many years, or over a lifetime—it is how they deal with life and often relates back to early-life experiences.

The positive potential opened up by Tall Yellow Top is a feeling of self-acceptance and self-worth, a sense of belonging, acceptance of others, and acceptance of All That Is. The transformation allows for forgiveness and acceptance, knowing that forgiveness does not condone or excuse bad behavior or abuse, but brings acceptance that it was what it was—we cannot stand in the shoes of another and truly understand why they chose to do what they did, but we can forgive them for what they did and did not do, and did and did not know, and therefore release ourselves from carrying the pain of it anymore.

Archangels

The highest resonance is between citrine and Archangel Jeremiel.

Archangel Jeremiel is one of the seven core archangels in ancient Judaic texts and is possibly best known for conducting life reviews with those who have newly crossed over from physical. However, Jeremiel also helps us understand prophetic dreams and enhances our innate intuition, guidance, and clairvoyance, and I have found a life review very helpful at various times of growth; we need not wait until we are no longer in physical. If we choose to review with the support of Jeremiel and the citrine synergistic combination, we are fully supported and protected as we review, understand, forgive, release old negative patterns, learn, and grow—and often it is the smallest of moments that hold the potential for greatest change.

Most of us can recount with ease the occasions of perceived injustices in our lives, and we are often so wrapped up in our story that we are unaware that the roots of entrenched negative patterning, attitudes, and beliefs are often planted in that which was not said or done, or a look that was given. It may not be our conscious memory of an occurrence or situation, but the small moments, long forgotten and sometimes not even acknowledged, that have sealed deep inside of us a negative behavior, thought process, reaction, or feeling that does not serve us well and continues to limit our ability to embrace a life well lived.

Periodically taking time out for a life evaluation with the support of Jeremiel, and especially with this citrine synergistic combination, can be exceptionally beneficial to our wellness and well-being. We change more than we are often aware as we experience life and grow. We are always fully supported and never called to deal with more than we are able to handle, despite feeling completely overburdened at times. When we willingly choose to undertake such a life review, we feel fearless and empowered by the process, and when we willingly and lovingly choose to release that which may have been brought to the surface to be released, we are gifted life-enhancing transformation and healing.

Whether we simply choose to connect for Divine guidance or participate in a life review, we are rewarded with clarity and inspiration of how best to proceed along the path that we have chosen at this time, or in relation to finding our life purpose. Crossroads are no longer seen as a difficulty but as an excellent opportunity to pause and review to consider that which would serve our highest good and the highest good of all—perhaps change is imminent, or perhaps confidently staying the course is all that is required. We are able to be thoughtful and reflective before moving forward with confidence and motivation, feeling the ease that comes from considered judgment, and the flow of momentum and all that it brings.

....

"Do you realize how often you do that…you set the bar high, very high, and then, just when you get close as you always seem to do, you then raise it again?! You've got self-sabotaging down to an art form and you don't even see it!"

This was sage advice I received a number of years ago from a straight-talking friend who is always there with unconditional kindness, compassion, and support…and that sometimes needs to be delivered in her unique no-nonsense way. She was retired from professional counseling and teaching various mind/body practices, and her assessment hit the mark. Although I felt I had accepted this advice and acknowledged and worked through this tendency, it was this moment that flashed back into memory when I first chose to do a life review with Jeremiel and the citrine synergistic combination. It was the opening for me to finally release the residual entrenched negative beliefs and memories that no longer served any good purpose.

Embracing the citrine synergistic combination has helped me in many areas, but ultimately to be able to feel heartfelt gratitude and appreciation for each who have played their part, and continue to play their part, in my life experience—for them being all that I needed them to be at the time— is life-changing and life-enhancing. I am so grateful for it all.

Meditation Practices

By choosing to quiet the mind with this citrine synergistic combination we feel revitalized, renewed, and protected, as the physical integrates with the spiritual, through the mental and emotional bodies. We embrace a sense of wonder at the abundance available to us in all areas—we are meant to prosper and we have awareness of our inherent value to All That Is. The infinite field of possibilities and potentialities is there for each of us. There is an elusive richness to a life that is regularly refreshed and aligned by quiet time alone in contemplation.

For the following meditations, please have at hand your crystal, essential oil, and crystal and flower essences. The crystal essence and combined flower essences may be taken in a single blend, or used separately, as is most convenient to you. The essential oil may certainly be vaporized in an oil burner to fill the meditation space, but as this is not always doable or convenient in some locations, please be assured that a few drops of essential oil on a tissue or handkerchief will serve you well at any time and in any location—whether meditating at home or in the park, or simply connecting in while waiting in line at the post office.

Sit in whatever way is comfortable for you—if seated in a chair, have your feet flat on the floor with no shoes. Ensure your back is straight by gently lifting your heart center. Relax your shoulders. Lengthen the back of the neck by slightly tilting the chin downward.

Take a couple of breaths and bring yourself to a place of quiet appreciation of this time that you are gifting you.

Meditation to Connect with the Citrine Synergy

Many will enjoy this as the most basic and "earthy" of the three meditations using the synergy of this combination. We will connect to the high vibrational energy that is created by the specific combination of these gifts from Mother Earth: citrine stone, sandalwood essential oil, and a blend of citrine, Wild Oat, and Tall Yellow Top essences. As always, it is all about the synergy of the combination. I use this meditation whenever I feel in need of the insight, support, and understanding that inevitably follow as I am re-energized and uplifted. To connect with the citrine synergy, you will need:

Citrine crystal

Sandalwood essential oil

Wild Oat and Tall Yellow Top flower essences

Citrine crystal essence

- Place four drops of the combined Wild Oat and Tall Yellow Top flower essences and citrine crystal essence under your tongue. Take a breath.

- Anoint the citrine crystal with a drop of sandalwood essential oil. Inhale the warm, mellow spicy aroma as you gently rub the oil into the stone, breathing slowly and deeply.

- Cup the citrine lightly in your hands—the fingertips of the right hand gently touch the base of the left palm—and rest your hands comfortably in your lap. Take a deep breath, softly close your eyes, and release any stress and unease with the exhalation.

- Feel the energy of the citrine as it fills your cupped hands—for example, it may feel tingly, effervescent, light, or heavy, or like your hands are suctioned together or they may expand apart during the session—there is no right way it should feel, and how it feels is right for you.

- Feel or imagine the energy moving up through your arms, and through to the heart center, from where it radiates out to fill your being, in whatever way feels right for you.

- Know that the synergy of the combination will revive, revitalize, heal, uplift, or enhance that which needs attention at this time.

- You may see the sunlit yellow of the citrine behind the closed eyes—maybe flashes, maybe dazzling color, or joyful golden color that fades in and out, as the energy of the citrine combination connects with, balances and expands through the various energy centers.

- Feel gratitude for any awareness or inspired thoughts that may come to you and let them go. Trust that all uplifting inspiration has settled into your being and will be there for you when you come out of the meditation.

- Feel the energy. Be in wonder of the synergy of these combined gifts from Mother Earth. Luxuriate in the harmony of connection; allow it to fill you, expand, nourish, and sustain you. Remain within that expansive grounded space for as long as you wish.

Meditation on the Essence of the Citrine Combination (with Affirmations)

Of the three citrine meditations, this is the most powerful for motivating and supporting change. We are revitalized and inspired to release that which no longer serves us, and we are energized to thrive in all areas and on all levels of our being. Again, it is all about the synergy of the combination that lifts the vibration of our physical, emotional, mental, and spiritual bodies, and the specific affirmations are an integral component of the synergy of this meditation practice. The affirmations allow and facilitate change in ways that continually surprise and delight me—the words remain unchanged each time, but the results are as different as I am each time I release, change, and grow, and then return to this inspired citrine affirmation practice.

- Please sit in your comfortable meditation position.

- Place four drops of your combined Wild Oat and Tall Yellow Top flower essences and citrine crystal essence under the tongue, anoint your citrine with a drop of sandalwood essential oil and inhale a few drops of sandalwood from a tissue or handkerchief while holding your stone in lightly cupped hands.

- Settle into the position, close your eyes, and take a long, slow, deep breath, releasing any tension on the exhale. Repeat with two more breaths.

- Take your awareness behind the eyebrow center. This is the third eye chakra. The color is deep indigo or purple. See yourself sitting in the middle of this space—the one in the middle who intuitively knows.

- Breathe.

- Take your awareness to the crown above you. See it layered with the petals of a closed lotus flower and imagine those petals unfolding, opening to pure positive energy and the infinite field of possibilities.

- Allow the pure white light to illuminate and enliven the deep indigo purple of this space. Feel the energy flood in and cascade through the physical body.

- Breathe.

- Repeat this statement to yourself. *I am revitalized and uplifted.*

- Breathe.

- Take your awareness to just below the navel center. This is the sacral chakra. The color is a rich orange. See the pelvic area as a golden bowl filled with the vibrant orange waters of creativity. You sit in the middle on a giant lotus leaf, perfectly balanced, fully supported.

- Breathe.

- No matter which way you choose to move, the liquid always returns to balance with you perfectly supported in the middle.

- Breathe.

- Repeat this statement to yourself. *I am gifted abundance and prosperity.*

- Breathe.

- Take your awareness to the chest center. This is the heart chakra—the middle chakra, that which bridges the upper three and lower three. The color is vibrant emerald or forest green. See yourself in the middle on a vibrant pink and white lotus flower atop a green lotus leaf. You are seated in your heart, the center of unconditional love.

- Breathe.

- See the heart center flooded with Divine energy from above as life-force energy rises to meet it from below. You are supported in Love from above and below.

- Repeat this statement to yourself. *I have infinite value.*

- Breathe.

- This powerful energy from your heart center floods down your arms and out through your hands to touch the world. You are fully supported and in your power as you choose to act from your heart.

- Repeat the full affirmation, feeling Spirit, or your innate Divinity, Higher Self, or beautiful Inner Being speaking to you. *You are revitalized and uplifted. You are abundant and prosperous in all areas of your life. You are of infinite value. You are energy being human.*

- Breathe. Remain in this space, feeling this space, for as long as it feels comfortable, or as long as your schedule allows.

- When you are ready, take a deep breath and bring your awareness back to the crown. See the petals of the lotus flower closing once again—yours to open at will, and close at will.

- Take another long, slow breath.

- Bring your awareness back into the body. Wiggle your toes and fingers, gently move your hands and your head, and open your eyes to bring your awareness fully back into this moment.

- Express gratitude for All That Is and the gift of grace ... and be aware that your Source is even more grateful for all that you are, and all that you are becoming. And so It is.

Meditation to Connect with Archangel Jeremiel, Higher Self, and Spirit Guides and Teachers

This simple meditation is often favored by those who already enjoy working with archangels, Spirit, guides, or teachers, but please remember that they are all aspects of our innate Divinity or essence. Whether you wish to connect with the energy of Archangel Jeremiel for release, insight, and clarity that comes from review, or whether you wish to connect to your own Inner Being, the synergy of the citrine combination will powerfully support your heartfelt intention to be present in the moment and to be open to allow that which is there for you to flow to you.

- Please sit in your comfortable meditation position.

- If you have a question or a situation with which you would like clarity or guiding support, or if you wish to undertake a life review, bring that to mind. Please mentally use words that feel right for you.

- Place four drops of your combined Wild Oat and Tall Yellow Top flower essences and citrine crystal essence under the tongue, anoint your citrine with a drop of sandalwood essential oil, inhale a few drops of the deep spicy sandalwood oil from a tissue or handkerchief and throughout the meditation if you feel inspired to do so, and hold your stone in lightly cupped hands.

- Settle into the position, close your eyes, and take a long, slow, deep breath, releasing any tension on the exhale. Repeat with two more breaths.

- Feeling relaxed, still, and present to the moment, please state your intentions. *I am present for all that is here for me. I am listening, and you are welcome.*

- Breathe and release any tension with a long exhalation.

- The soft sound of the breath mirrors the tranquil space of silence where inner peace and harmony are found. Feel the breath, hear the breath, and allow for any awareness of connection that follows.

- Feel deep appreciation and gratitude for this time of connection to a Divine messenger, teacher, or aspect of Oneness, and come out of the meditation whenever you are ready.

Please know that no matter what you feel or do not feel during the meditation, any question you have asked has been answered, any clarity you are seeking has been forthcoming, and any connection you desired has been facilitated by the synergy of the high vibrational combination of citrine crystal, sandalwood essential oil, and the citrine, Wild Oat, and Tall Yellow Top essence blend, and Archangel Jeremiel. Your conscious awareness of renewed vitality and abundance in all areas, appreciation of the value inherent in all that you are and all that you choose to do, and your sense of inspiration have been awakened and heightened. If this is not a familiar practice for you, please be reassured that enhanced connection is always facilitated and clarity and answers always provided. Sometimes guidance will flow into your consciousness during the practice, sometimes you will be inspired to pick up a particular book, or turn onto a certain radio or television channel, or bump into someone as you go about your day. The answers and clarity always flow, but we do not always get to micromanage how they come to us. Indeed, trusting in our inherent guidance will always deliver that which we seek in the quickest, most direct, and life-enhancing way ... we just need to trust.

Remember, it is in the smallest of moments that miracles happen and the revitalizing review and release of Jeremiel and associated teachers and guides, including your Higher Self, facilitated through the synergy of the citrine combination is indeed inspired.

Fluorite

Traditional Chakra Association
Heart (4th) • Third Eye (6th) • Crown (7th)
Higher Crown (8th)

Main Applications
Renewal • Alignment • Attunement • Infinite Choice

Synergistic Combination
Crystal: Fluorite
Essential Oil: Neroli
Flower Essences: Agrimony and Macrocarpa
Archangel: Raphael

This powerfully protective and healing stone comes in clear, purple, violet, and green, as well as yellow, blue, and pink—the colors can be vibrant, or soft and pale. It is a stone of order, progress, and fulfillment, and a wonderful healing stone that constantly fills me with wonder.

Fluorite has been used for its healing properties and beauty across the ages: the ancient Egyptians and the Chinese used it for carving, protection and healing; and in more recent centuries, Europeans took it as a gem elixir, or crystal essence, for kidney disorders.

This extremely protective and healing stone puts things in order and supports our progress on multiple levels by clearing, cleansing, dissolving, dispelling, stabilizing, and purifying fixed and negative energy patterns that restrict and limit our potential. Fluorite is particularly protective on the psychic level and will stop psychic manipulation and unhelpful thought patterns. Fluorite heightens awareness of our innate intuition and confidence to trust our inner knowing. It helps us open to the infinite field of possibilities and potentialities, thereby enhancing our creativity in the physical.

Fluorite attracts, absorbs, and dissolves negative vibrations and helps us become more open to the resonance of other crystals. It is an excellent meditation stone. It also absorbs electromagnetic energy and will change the negative into positive.

Known as the Genius Stone, fluorite makes an excellent learning aid as it enables us to process what we are learning and integrate it with what we already know. Concentration and decision-making are enhanced.

Fluorite is the third stone in the group known as the Creative Triad: pyrite for the spark of inspiration, calcite for releasing resistance and easing transition, and fluorite for the energy of fulfillment and the final stage of the creative process—manifestation.

How Fluorite Facilitates Well-Being

- Fluorite grounds and integrates the physical with the spiritual—it clears and stabilizes the aura, reorganizing and balancing the physical, mental, and emotional bodies.

- It is an excellent meditation stone and can be particularly useful with other stones as it enhances our ability to be open and receive the other energies.

- This powerful stone will draw, absorb, purify, and dispel all types of negative energies and stress.

- Fluorite will dissolve and undo fixed negative behavioral patterns, open the subconscious and unconscious, and bring suppressed negative feelings to the surface to be resolved—enhancing our ability to adapt with increased self-confidence.

- It stabilizes our emotions and we clearly understand the impact of our thoughts and emotions on the physical body—we appreciate the importance of balance. Fluorite improves both mental and physical coordination and balance—another reminder of the wholeness of it all.

....

I'm sure many can relate to that feeling of *If only I'd known then what I know now!* This best encapsulates how I feel about this wonderful fluorite synergistic combination because, although I now use it regularly whenever I wish to enhance my connection to Spirit and Archangel Raphael, I did not have this knowledge in my earlier days as a healer.

My work with natural therapies, energy, and the mind/body connection has been an evolving passion that, with hindsight, seems to be as old as me, but when I was first qualified to practice, my deepest fears of disappointing others, not being good enough, and lack of self-worth, all rose to the surface—and to compound my fears, my first client was someone with whom I had an emotional connection and who had long been dealing with an autoimmune condition and had suffered a number of disappointments with other practitioners.

As much as I believed that it was not my job to heal the world and understand that I could only ever facilitate healing in partnership with the client, when I shared the space with my early clients, all my knowing and understanding went straight out the window. Thoughts such as, *What if I do something that makes it worse?...I can't do this!...I don't know enough*...filled my head as soon as the clients left the clinic.

This beautiful fluorite synergistic combination would have been perfect for my emotional exhaustion, my ever-hidden mental torture, and the tossing and turning at night. Knowing what I know now, life as a privately fearful and intense practitioner would have been very different if I'd been able to access the synergy of the fluorite combination to clear these entrenched beliefs that were not serving me well.

Interestingly, the healing I have been privileged enough to facilitate since the early days would possibly have been no different as I have been blessed with happy clients. However the ease with which it was delivered, and the toll on me mentally and emotionally, and inevitably physically, would have been very different. Enjoying and embracing heightened awareness of my innate connection now supports my intention to serve the highest good in all that I do, and all that I serve—and therefore the highest good is served with ease and flow.

Essential Oils, Flower Essences, and Spirit Connection

Fluorite has been a much-loved stone across the ages, but its powerful potential is magnified exponentially in combination. When we treat ourselves to the synergy that results in the following specific combinations, we allow ourselves to be surprised and delighted by the possible transformation available to us.

Essential Oils

Neroli, rosewood, and angelica have been cited by other practitioners as resonating with fluorite, particularly with the eighth or higher crown chakra in subtle aromatherapy. However, the highest resonance is between fluorite and neroli essential oil. Traditionally, fluorite is used with the heart, third eye, crown, and higher crown chakras, but this power combination works effectively and synergistically to harmonize the whole being whether the crystal is placed on the body, held, worn, carried in the pocket, or placed nearby.

The eighth, or higher crown, chakra is the center of the Higher Self, the one who "sits in the middle and knows" as poet Robert Frost beautifully described—it is that stillness within from where we reach out to the Divine. The energy is pure and expansive and therefore it should be no surprise that the oil that fully harmonizes with its purity and radiance is that extracted from the pure white blossoms of the bitter orange (*Citrus aurantium*): neroli.

This precious essential oil is extracted by steam distillation of the fragrant flowers, as well as by the time-consuming enfleurage method using animal fat. Like jasmine and rose oils, neroli is not inexpensive to produce, with one hundred kilograms of flowers yielding one liter of the precious essential oil.

The delicate, pale yellow neroli oil is profoundly calming to the physical body and will purify any environment: use it in a purifying bath or in a burner to purify your meditation space and allow for healing, or simply place a few drops on a tissue to inhale for immediate tranquility and reassuring reconnection.

This refreshing, relaxing, calming, and uplifting oil will calm a charged emotional state, uplift from anxiety and depression, and help with confusion, poor concentration, apathy, despair, despondency, lethargy, fear, irritability, jealousy, panic, shock, and restlessness to mention but a few of its applications.

Neroli is a "specific" for stress in aromatherapy and therefore considered first in any essential oil blend—neroli and lavender make an excellent soothing blend. Indeed, amethyst and fluorite synergistic combinations would be an excellent "go-to" combination in times of stress.

On the emotional barometer, neroli aligns with the spiritual body transforming the negative feelings of no choice into an expansive awareness of the unlimited choices that are available to us. This delightful fragrance bridges the subtle bodies, bringing renewal and alignment that encourages awareness of consequences, and considered and empowered choices. We are empowered to change and that is no small feat!

Flower Essences

The highest resonance is between fluorite and Agrimony Bach Flower and Macrocarpa Australian Bush Flower Essences.

Agrimony Bach Flower Essence is the remedy for those who are oversensitive to outside influences: the sad clown; the one who hides their inner torture and pain behind a mask of cheerfulness or dismissiveness; the one who agonizes over situations. The negative agrimony state is the ultimate minimizer, minimizing their concerns; the one who outwardly shows all is well when underneath all is far from well—the mask is firmly in place or never far from reach.

The negative agrimony person is overly sensitive to what is happening, and not only has a strong desire for constant harmony but will feel great stress with any discord. It is not unusual for these sensitive beings to seek solace in food, drugs, alcohol, or similar addictions in order to relieve the stress of hiding their inner pain. Agrimony offers valuable support in the treatment of addiction.

Any kind of stress in the body—physical, mental, or emotional—suppresses the immune system and inhibits the physical body's natural healing processes. A compromised immune system leaves the body vulnerable to disease, and once the physical body succumbs, the physical stress of illness then restricts the body's ability to recover. Meditation is a powerful way to alleviate stress and stimulate our immune system; meditating with the healing fluorite synergistic combination facilitates healing emotionally, mentally, and physically as immune function is enhanced and the body's innate healing systems are rebooted into action. The physical body is a magnificent mechanism and a wonderful indicator of choices that are not serving us well, and I am in constant wonder of its forgiving nature when we choose to change.

The potential agrimony transformation brings heartfelt inner joy and a sense of discrimination, discernment, and genuine optimism. There is ease of integration of all that we are and acceptance of both the highs and lows of a life well lived; we toss the mask away, see life for what it is, no longer sweat the small stuff (and see that it's all small stuff), and genuinely smile at contrasts that arise when we choose to embrace life.

Macrocarpa is the Australian Bush Flower Essence that offers wonderful support during convalescence and is excellent when we are feeling tired and exhausted, or completely burnt out—those times when we take on too much and send the adrenals into overdrive. Our adrenals govern our innate fight/flight response, and constant adrenal stress results in a physical body that lacks vitality, has a weakened immune system, and suffers stress on all levels—unaddressed stress, whether it be physical, mental, or emotional, is the often unacknowledged root cause of all disharmony in the physical body and chronic illness.

This remedy recharges and revitalizes our life force, our innate vitality, and, when combined with meditation, enhances our ability to tune into and align with the limitless source of physical, mental, and emotional wellness and well-being available to us.

Archangels

The highest resonance is between fluorite and Archangel Raphael.

Archangel Raphael is a powerful healer, and indeed, he is one of the four archangels who particularly facilitate healing: Michael, Raphael, Uriel, and Haniel. Raphael's healing can come direct for us or be directed to others, as we request, and even those not open to healing are comforted by his energy—comfort that relieves stress and anxiety, and therefore facilitates healing.

He brings valuable support to those who are dealing with addictions and helps with clearing any type of negativity. Raphael's all-loving energy supports any decision to willingly and lovingly release negativity or fear—there is always a void when fear is released and Raphael will pump in loving energy to fill that void. We come to understand and accept our innate dualities and choose to release negativity; balance is restored with the inflow of pure positive and loving energy, and we enjoy a life richly rewarded by the healing power of love. We feel clear and in tune, joyful and supported to choose from the smorgasbord of life.

Raphael helps heal issues relating to physical sight, as well as enhancing spiritual sight by opening the third eye, improving clairvoyance, and enhancing our spiritual connection. Raphael also guides and supports those of us who are healers and travelers—protecting both physical and spiritual travelers in a way that embraces order, harmony, and grace.

....

There was much study and many healing and spiritual avenues explored before I was in a position to bring all of these tools together in these synergistic crystal combinations. Since using the fluorite synergistic combination and practice, I have come to know that Archangel Raphael has been there supporting me on all my travels.

My experiences are no less relevant to all those who care for or support another, or struggle with hidden fears and doubts in life and along their spiritual paths, as well as other healers and practitioners who find themselves struggling from time to time. Divine support is constant and ever-present, but we are also gifted free will and we get to choose. We need only ask and be open to it if we wish to receive; we are free to live our lives however we choose.

What wonderful modeling our non-physical friends offer us: they offer unconditional love and support but they also practice non-interference. We need only to ask, to participate, and it is there. Likewise, as much as we in physical may wish to help or interfere to try to "fix" or make something or someone "better," we can only be of assistance if and when asked. There is just no sense in answering a question that has not been asked: at best, the answer is not received; at worst, the answer is upsetting to the other and resistance to change increased. When we are in tune, facilitated by the synergy of this combination and Raphael, we have no need to fix that which does not need fixing.

Meditation Practices

By choosing to quiet the mind with this fluorite synergistic combination we open up to be refreshed, renewed, realigned, and rebalanced, as the physical integrates with the spiritual, through the mental and emotional bodies. We embrace a sense of wonder at the innate order, balance, and perfection in it all. The infinite field of possibilities and potentialities is there for each of us. There is an elusive richness to a life that is regularly refreshed and aligned by quiet time alone in contemplation.

For the following meditations, please have at hand your crystal, essential oil, and crystal and flower essences. The crystal essence and combined flower essences may be taken in a single blend, or used separately, as is most convenient to you. The essential oil may certainly be vaporized in an oil burner to fill the meditation space, but as this is not always doable or convenient in some locations, please be assured that a few drops of essential oil on a tissue or handkerchief will serve you well at any time and in any location—whether meditating at home or in public gardens, or simply connecting in while waiting for some pain to pass, or some ticket line to move.

Sit in whatever way is comfortable for you—if seated in a chair, have your feet flat on the floor with no shoes. Ensure your back is straight by gently lifting your heart center. Relax your shoulders. Lengthen the back of the neck by slightly tilting the chin downward.

Take a couple of breaths and bring yourself to a place of quiet appreciation of this time that you are gifting you.

Meditation to Connect with the Fluorite Synergy

I have no doubt that many of you will find this the simplest and "earthiest" of the three meditations using fluorite in combination. In this meditation, we connect to the high vibrational energy that is created by the specific combination of these gifts from Mother Earth: fluorite stone, neroli essential oil, and a blend of fluorite, Agrimony, and Macrocarpa essences. As always, it is all about the synergy of the combination. I use this meditation whenever I feel in need of the guiding support, comfort, connection, and healing that inevitably follow as I am calmed and uplifted. To connect with the fluorite synergy, you will need:

Fluorite crystal

Neroli essential oil

Agrimony and Macrocarpa flower essences

Fluorite crystal essence

- Place four drops of the combined Agrimony and Macrocarpa flower essences and fluorite crystal essence under your tongue. Take a breath.

- Anoint the beautiful fluorite crystal with a drop of neroli essential oil. Inhale the delicately refreshing and purifying fragrance as you gently rub the oil into the stone, breathing slowly and deeply.

- Cup the fluorite lightly in your hands—the fingertips of the right hand gently touch the base of the left palm—and rest your hands comfortably in your lap. Take a deep breath, softly close your eyes, and release any stress and unease with the exhalation.

- Feel the energy of the fluorite as it fills your cupped hands— for example, it may feel tingling, effervescent, light, heavy, or like your hands are suctioned together or they may expand apart during the session—there is no right way it should feel, and how it feels is right for you.

- Feel or imagine the energy moving up through your arms, and through to the heart center, from where it radiates out to fill your entire being, in whatever way feels right for you.

- Know that the synergy of the combination will align, heal, uplift, calm, or enhance that which needs attention at this time.

- You may see the colors ranging from soft or vibrant green through blue to purple and white of the fluorite behind the closed eyes—maybe flashes, maybe swirling or fading colors, as the energy of the fluorite combination connects with, attunes and expands through the various energy centers.

- Feel gratitude for any awareness, knowing or inspired thoughts that may come to you and let them go. Trust that all uplifting inspiration and healing has settled into your being and will be there for you when you come out of the meditation.

- Feel the energy. Be in wonder of the synergy of these combined gifts from Mother Earth. Luxuriate in the alignment and support of connection, and allow it to fill you, nourish you, and sustain you. Remain within that expansive grounded space for as long as you wish.

Meditation on the Essence of the Fluorite Combination (with Affirmations)

The most powerful of the three fluorite meditations for supporting change, this meditation opens us to the choices that flow from a sincere intention to release that which no longer supports us, and act from a heart in alignment with all that we are. Again, it is all about the synergy of the combination that lifts the vibration of our physical, emotional, mental, and spiritual bodies, and the specific affirmations are an integral component of the synergy of this meditation practice. The affirmations allow and facilitate change in ways that continually surprise and delight me—the words remain unchanged each time, but the results are as different as I am each time I change and grow, and then return to this inspired fluorite affirmation practice.

- Please sit in your comfortable meditation position.

- Place four drops of your combined Agrimony and Macrocarpa flower essences and fluorite crystal essence under the tongue, anoint your fluorite with a drop of neroli essential oil and inhale a few drops of neroli from a tissue or handkerchief while holding your stone in lightly cupped hands.

- Settle into the position, close your eyes, and take a long, slow, deep breath, releasing any tension on the exhale. Repeat with two more breaths.

- Take your awareness behind the eyebrow center. This is the third eye chakra. The color is deep indigo or purple. See yourself sitting in the middle of this space—the one in the middle who intuitively knows.

- Breathe.

- Take your awareness to the crown above you. See it layered with the petals of a closed lotus flower and imagine those petals unfolding, opening to pure positive energy and the infinite field of possibilities.

- Allow the pure white light to illuminate and enliven the deep indigo purple of this space. Feel the energy flood in and cascade through the physical body.

- Breathe.

- Repeat this statement to yourself. *I am refreshed and renewed, aligned and in tune.*

- Breathe.

- Take your awareness to just below the navel center. This is the sacral chakra. The color is a rich orange. See the pelvic area as a golden bowl filled with the vibrant orange waters of creativity. You sit in the middle on a giant lotus leaf, perfectly balanced, fully supported.

- Breathe.

- No matter which way you choose to move, the liquid always returns to balance with you perfectly supported in the middle.

- Breathe.

- Repeat this statement to yourself. *I am gifted infinite choices.*

- Breathe.

- Take your awareness to the chest center. This is the heart chakra—the middle chakra, that which bridges the upper three and lower three. The color is vibrant emerald or forest green. See yourself in the middle on a vibrant pink and white lotus flower atop a green lotus leaf. You are seated in your heart, the center of unconditional love.

- Breathe.

- See the heart center flooded with Divine energy from above as life-force energy rises to meet it from below. You are supported in Love from above and below.

- Repeat this statement to yourself. *I am fully supported.*

- Breathe.

- This powerful energy from your heart center floods down your arms and out through your hands to touch the world. You are fully supported and in your power as you choose to act from your heart.

- Repeat the full affirmation, feeling Spirit, your innate Divinity, Higher Self, or beautiful Inner Being speaking to you. *You are refreshed and renewed, aligned and in tune. Your choices are infinite, and you are fully supported. You are energy being human.*

- Breathe. Remain in this space, feeling this space, for as long as it feels comfortable, or as long as your schedule allows.

- When you are ready, take a deep breath and bring your awareness back to the crown. See the petals of the lotus flower closing once again—yours to open at will, and close at will.

- Take another long, slow breath.

- Bring your awareness back into the body. Wiggle your toes and fingers, gently move your hands and your head, and open your eyes to bring your awareness fully back into this moment.

- Express gratitude for All That Is and the gift of grace … and be aware that your Source is even more grateful for all that you are, and all that you are becoming. And so It is.

Meditation to Connect with Archangel Raphael, Higher Self, and Spirit Guides and Teachers

This simple meditation is often favored by those who already enjoy working with archangels, Spirit, guides, or teachers, but please remember that they are all aspects of our innate Divinity or essence. Whether you wish to connect with the energy of Archangel Raphael for support, comfort, guidance, and realignment, or whether you wish to connect to your own Inner Being, the synergy of the fluorite combination will powerfully support your heartfelt intention to be present in the moment and to be open to allow that which is there for you to flow to you.

- Please sit in your comfortable meditation position.

- If you have a question or a situation with which you would like clarity, support, or healing, bring that to mind.

- Place four drops of your combined Agrimony and Macrocarpa flower essences and fluorite crystal essence under the tongue, anoint your fluorite with a drop of neroli essential oil, inhale a few drops of the expansive and purifying neroli oil from a tissue or handkerchief and throughout the meditation if you feel inspired to do so, and hold your stone in lightly cupped hands.

- Settle into the position, close your eyes, and take a long, slow, deep breath, releasing any tension on the exhale. Repeat with two more breaths.

- Feeling relaxed, still, and present to the moment, please state your intentions. *I am present for all that is here for me. I am listening, and you are welcome.*

- Breathe and release any tension with a long exhalation.

- The soft sound of the breath mirrors the tranquil space of silence where inner peace and harmony are found. Feel the breath, hear the breath, and allow for any awareness of connection that follows.

- Feel deep appreciation and gratitude for this time of connection to a Divine messenger, teacher, or aspect of Oneness, and come out of the meditation whenever you are ready.

Please know that no matter what you feel or do not feel during the meditation, any question you have asked has been answered, any clarity you are seeking has been forthcoming, and any connection you desired has been facilitated by the synergy of the high vibrational combination of fluorite crystal, neroli essential oil, and the fluorite, Agrimony, and Macrocarpa essence blend, and Archangel Raphael. Your conscious awareness of the comfort and strength from renewal, alignment, attunement, and the infinite choices available to each of us when we are in tune with all that we are, have been awakened and heightened. If this is not a familiar practice for you, please be reassured that enhanced connection is always facilitated and clarity and answers always provided. Sometimes guidance will flow into your consciousness during the practice, sometimes you will be inspired to pick up a particular book, or turn onto a certain radio or television channel, or bump into someone as you go about your day. The answers and clarity always flow, but we do not always get to micromanage how they come to us. Indeed, trusting in our inherent guidance will always deliver that which we seek in the quickest, most direct, and life-enhancing way ... we just need to trust.

Remember, it is in the smallest of moments that miracles happen and the healing and protection as you travel with Raphael and associated teachers and guides, including your Higher Self, facilitated through the synergy of the fluorite combination is indeed inspired.

Jasper, Red

Traditional Chakra Association
Base (1st) • Sacral (2nd)

Main Applications
Clarity • Simplicity • Ease and Flow • Integrity

Synergistic Combination
Crystal: Red Jasper
Essential Oil: Jasmine
Flower Essences: Gentian and Sturt Desert Rose
Archangel: Raguel

One of the oldest recorded gemstones, jasper is known as the "supreme nurturer," protecting, supporting, and sustaining during times of stress. This wonderful stone sustains us, supports us, and gives us a sense of peace, acceptance, and wholeness—there is no separation. Jasper comes in red, brown, yellow, green, blue, and purple—all help restore balance to various parts of the body by balancing the emotional body.

However, it is often noted that change can be slow when treating with jasper, and this can deter some from working with it—but red and brecciated jaspers are such powerfully nurturing and sustaining stones that I choose to not be without them. Brecciated jasper is red jasper veined with hematite. Jasper may need to be used longer than other stones, but a large piece of red jasper in a room will absorb negative energy, including environmental and electromagnetic pollution and radiation. Clearing a space in this way is not only nurturing, it also enhances energetic practices such as dowsing—one of my crystal pendulums is the weighty but decisive red jasper.

Jasper aligns all of the chakras; red jasper resonates powerfully with the base chakras, and in particular with the sacral chakra, our Hara or Zen Knowing Mind, balancing and harmonizing the yin and yang, the feminine and the masculine, and strengthening our connection to Mother Earth. It attunes our physical, mental, and emotional bodies with the spiritual realm, bringing us into alignment with All That Is.

Jasper brings determination, strength, and focus to whatever we choose to be or do—we find the courage, assertiveness, and tenacity to come to terms with issues or problems, and we are able to deal with situations with integrity and in a manner congruent with our own higher truth. We are aided by clarity of thought and quick thinking that is decisive, inspiration and imagination that give birth to ideas, vitality to action our passion, and tenacity and organization to efficiently see the project through to completion. We are supremely nurtured, indeed.

Red jasper balances and heals physical, mental, and emotional pain: it grounds and stabilizes us; it gently stimulates on all levels of our being; it balances and harmonizes the emotions, and it energizes the system. It offers powerful support and protection against those things that do not serve us well, and eases emotional stress and struggle. Calming, harmonizing red jasper makes an excellent "worry bead."

How Red Jasper Facilitates Well-Being

- Red jasper brings courage and determination to all that we choose to be and do.

- It enhances our ability to be assertive, set and strengthen personal boundaries, and come to grips with any problem.

- It supports quick thinking, decision-making, and the ability to organize and manage projects.

- Red jasper stimulates the imagination and creativity and promotes an ability to bring ideas to fruition.

- It helps with dream recall when placed under the pillow; it is helpful for rebirthing with the gentle stimulation to the base chakras.

- Red jasper cleanses, detoxifies, and stabilizes the aura.

. . . .

This is my combination of ease and flow. It facilitates immediate calming energy to wash through me whenever I feel old fear-based worrywart tendencies stirring inside from something another has said or done.

No matter how cherished our relationships, we all have those who push our buttons—they can be close to us or be transient travelers who stay just long enough to have an effect. Indeed, I'm sure we are *all* designated button-pushers for at least one other person. Button-pushers seem to zero in on our weak spots; there's no hiding from what they stir within us. It can happen anytime, but the most distressing moments are so often triggered by annual or anniversary get-togethers with family or friends that hold all the baggage from past events.

This nurturing red jasper synergistic combination continually supports my intention to live in integrity, to hold true to that which feels right for me at any given time, and to do no harm and allow others equal respect. The feeling of taking a breath, knowing that I am supported, protected, and have nothing to prove—that I can just be—brings a stillness inside that settles and empowers me to be with those I enjoy, celebrate the occasion, and walk away with no emotional baggage or barbs.

I embrace self-responsibility and self-determination. I no longer abdicate responsibility for my own joy to another; and opportunities abound and unfold for me through the synchronicities of life.

So, when circumstances bring the button-pushers into my world, I have a choice: I can engage with them, I can move away, or I can bring awareness to the feelings that are being disturbed and the gifted opportunity to release and let go. I can feel genuine appreciation and gratitude to those who have triggered an opportunity to release that which no longer serves me. I can actually bless the button-pushers! They are our greatest teachers.

Life and life's lessons do not need to feel as hard or painful as I sometimes made them in the past—deep inside me there has always been a yearning for simplicity and ease and flow. These three little words, *ease and flow,* instantly calm me at all times of stress. The red jasper synergistic combination eases the way forward and supports this outcome … and blessing the button-pushers feels awesome!

Essential Oils, Flower Essences, and Spirit Connection

Red jasper has been embraced across time and cultures to nurture and empower, but the potentialities and possibilities that it can open for us are transformed when it is used in combination. When we choose to immerse ourselves in the synergy of the following combinations, we gift ourselves a life that is authentic and flows with ease.

Essential Oils

The highest resonance is between red jasper and jasmine essential oil. Traditionally, red jasper is used with the base and sacral chakras, but this power combination works effectively and synergistically to harmonize the whole being whether the crystal is placed on the body, held, worn, carried in the pocket, or placed nearby.

Jasmine (*Jasminum officinale*), originally a native of Northern India and Persia, was introduced into Europe in the seventeenth century. The name is derived from the Persian *Yasmin,* meaning "gift from God." Persian women would soak the exquisitely fragrant flowers in sesame oil to massage into their skin and hair; likewise it was prized by the Chinese, who used it for cosmetic and medicinal purposes. Garlands of jasmine symbolize respect in Buddhist ceremonies.

The deep mahogany-brown essential oil is extracted from the flower petals, which are picked in the early evening after the sun has gone down to capture the full intensity of aroma. Jasmine, like neroli, is one of the more precious essential oils. The labor-intensive extraction method of enfleurage is required to extract the essential oil from the fragile petals, and thousands of flowers (some estimate 8,000 flowers) are required to produce just one gram of oil.

Jasmine uplifts, calms, and relaxes every layer of our being. The exotic aroma permeates the layers of the subtle bodies to touch us deep in our soul; fear is dispelled as we reconnect to Spirit and the Divine knowing deep inside each of us. The sensual beauty of jasmine dissolves fears, and seemingly insurmountable emotional challenges are dispersed, as we find the stillness within, listen with an open heart, and trust our Inner Being to guide us. We are uplifted and inspired by a deep faith that is not blind, but that which comes from self-awareness and connection to our Higher Self.

On the emotional barometer, jasmine aligns with the spiritual body, transforming the negative fearful emotional state into one that is fearless and trusting. Anxiety and depression, and feelings of dejection and self-doubt, are dissipated as we are uplifted and calmed into a place of quiet assuredness. We move into energetic integrity, feel supported to embrace all that we are, and become gently assertive as we fearlessly make choices with awareness and intention to serve the highest good.

Flower Essences

The highest resonance is between red jasper and Gentian Bach Flower and Sturt Desert Rose Australian Bush Flower Essences.

Gentian Bach Flower Essence is for those who are easily discouraged and worry when things go wrong. The negative Gentian state is disconnected from Higher Self and feels dis-Spirited, unsupported, fearful, and separate from the whole.

Even the most inspired and passionate natural practitioner can drop into this negative state and, in their heart of hearts, harbor some doubt as to their efficacy of a treatment with a particular client, despite proven efficacy and success in the past. Gentian helps us return to faith in our hearts—not blind faith, but the powerful faith of the positive skeptic, one who is intellectually strong and balanced as they question and discriminate, and not one who dis-believingly questions everything with fear and negativity in their hearts.

The potential Gentian transformation is one who can see light in the darkest of moments and uplift others. There is a quiet assuredness that comes from appreciation that problems can always be overcome and there is no such thing as failure, as we have given it our best. There are always lessons along the way, experiences to be had, and paths to be explored. There is great relief and ease when one lives in integrity and with an understanding that we need only do the best that we can at the time—and today our best may be different from our best tomorrow.

Obstacles are no longer insurmountable, and no job too big; optimism replaces pessimism; self-belief replaces self-doubt; self-confidence and an inner conviction that the task is doable replaces lack of faith.

Sturt Desert Rose Australian Bush Flower Essence helps us to release guilt; we experience life, we do the best we can at the time with what we know, and we learn and grow. We must realize that although choices may be different next time, at the time, we did the best we could.

Guilt is one of the most soul-destroying feelings we can have, and so easily manifests in deeply entrenched low self-esteem and negative behaviors. The two leading indicators for using this remedy are guilt and low self-esteem. Many relate peer pressure to children and teenagers, but we can succumb to peer pressure at any age as we step out of our integrity and act contrary to our own truth and sense of justice—and, of course, the guilt when we are no longer true to ourselves is immediate and intense and can gnaw away at us over time. Guilt plays right into the hands of our inner critic, ever ready to replay the event like a rerun of a B-movie, and thereby strengthen its impact and further chip away at self-esteem. It becomes an insidious cycle and, as with everything in our lives, it is all intertwined, all part of the same energy system.

The potential positive outcome from Sturt Desert Rose is strength and courage to remain true to our Inner Being, true to self, and to live in integrity according to our inner convictions that serve us well, and the highest good of all—and, for me, to be congruent with all that we are and All That Is, is to live a life with ease and flow.

Archangels

The highest resonance is between red jasper and Archangel Raguel.

Archangel Raguel brings loving and enthusiastic energy that harmonizes and brings order to our lives and facilitates dispute resolution for the highest good. Raguel's name means "friend of God," and he is traditionally known as the archangel who harmonizes and organizes the angelic realm in keeping with Divine order. He certainly creates harmony within relationships and helps us make decisions that involve others for the highest good of all concerned.

Raguel motivates, counsels, energizes, empowers, protects, and so much more—and for me is a spiritual champion and life coach when I need one. His powerful energy will never interfere—as always, our free will is paramount—but once asked, he guides us to considered decisions that bring fairness and justice to all concerned.

We are supported to embrace the simplicity and ease of a life lived with acceptance of self-responsibility, self-respect, and self-awareness, and a practice of non-attachment to outcome of how things should and should not be. He brings love, joy, balance, moderation, and inner peace. There is ease and flow to our path, abundance of choice, harmony, clarity, awareness, and understanding. We take responsibility for our choices, and stand in integrity as we make decisions that bring the most harmonious outcome, and so serve the higher good.

....

I find the red jasper synergistic combination offers potent support; I am able to continue on my chosen path with ease and flow. We come into this life with no rule book or map to navigate clear passage. Relationships come in all shapes and forms, and some are old and some are fleeting. We have relationships with fellow travelers and with ourselves; relationships with our environment and the world we create; and relationships to thoughts, feelings, and things that, for whatever reason, feel important to us—and all of our relationships have potential for great joy and great pain. But inherent in each is the potential for change, refining perspective, letting go, and embracing and nurturing that which we hold dear.

There is simplicity to my life these days, even at the busiest of times. I have learned to set boundaries, some are malleable but most are not, and taking time each morning to connect to All That Is, my Inner Being, and that which supports me is absolutely non-negotiable. It is that which nurtures me, sustains me, and empowers me. At the end of the day, I am comfortable that I have sought to do no harm and walked with an intention to choose for the highest good and act from my heart.

Meditation Practices

By choosing to quiet the mind with the nurturing red jasper synergistic combination we open to the clarity, simplicity, ease, and flow available to all of us, as the physical integrates with the spiritual, through the mental and emotional bodies. We embrace a sense of wonder at the innate order, balance, and perfection in it all when we are in integrity. The infinite field of possibilities and potentialities is there for each of us. There is an elusive richness and simplicity to a life that is regularly refreshed and aligned by quiet time alone in contemplation.

For the following meditations, please have at hand your crystal, essential oil, and crystal and flower essences. The crystal essence and combined flower essences may be taken in a single blend, or used separately, as is most convenient to you. The essential oil may certainly be vaporized in an oil burner to fill the meditation space, but as this is not always doable or convenient in some locations, please be assured that a few drops of essential oil on a tissue or handkerchief will serve you well at any time and in any place—whether meditating at home or in the park, or simply connecting in while waiting in line at the supermarket.

Sit in whatever way is comfortable for you—if seated in a chair, have your feet flat on the floor with no shoes. Ensure your back is straight by gently lifting your heart center. Relax your shoulders. Lengthen the back of the neck by slightly tilting the chin downward.

Take a couple of breaths and bring yourself to a place of quiet appreciation of this time that you are gifting you.

Meditation to Connect with the Red Jasper Synergy

This is perhaps the simplest and "earthiest" of the three red jasper meditations. In this meditation, we connect to the high vibrational energy that is created by the specific combination of these gifts from Mother Earth: red jasper stone, jasmine essential oil, and a blend of red jasper, Gentian, and Sturt Desert Rose essences. As always, it is all about the synergy of the combination. I use this meditation whenever I feel in need of the stability, simplicity, and sense of ease that inevitably follow as I am grounded and uplifted. To connect with the red jasper synergy you will need:

Red jasper crystal

Jasmine essential oil

Gentian and Sturt Desert Rose flower essences

Red jasper crystal essence

- Place four drops of the combined Gentian and Sturt Desert Rose flower essences and red jasper crystal essence under your tongue. Take a breath.

- Anoint the red jasper with a drop of jasmine essential oil. Inhale the uplifting exotic aroma as you gently rub the oil into the stone, breathing slowly and deeply.

- Cup the nurturing red jasper lightly in your hands—the fingertips of the right hand gently touch the base of the left palm—and rest your hands comfortably in your lap. Take a deep breath, softly close your eyes, and release any worry and stress with the exhalation.

- Feel the energy of the red jasper as it fills your cupped hands—for example, it may feel tingling, effervescent, light, heavy, or like your hands are suctioned together or they may expand apart during the session—there is no right way it should feel, and how it feels is right for you.

- Feel or imagine the energy moving up through your arms, through to your beautiful heart center, and radiating out to fill your being in whatever way feels right for you.

- Know that the synergy of the combination will nurture, stabilize, heal, open, or enhance that which needs attention at this time.

- You may see the earthy red of the red jasper behind the closed eyes—maybe flashes, maybe an expansive desert of color, or color that fades in and out, as the energy of the red jasper combination connects with, balances, strengthens, and expands through the various energy centers.

- You are nurtured and balanced in this space. There is simplicity and ease in this space. Feel gratitude for any clarity that may flow to you and let it go. Trust that any insight, inspiration, or awareness has settled into your being and will be with you, guiding you with a sense of ease and flow, when you come out of the meditation.

- Feel the energy. Be in wonder of the synergy of these combined gifts from Mother Earth. Luxuriate in the stability, simplicity, and clarity of connection, and allow it to nourish you and sustain you. Remain within that grounded expansive space for as long as you wish.

Meditation on the Essence of the Red Jasper Combination (with Affirmations)

This is the most powerful of the three red jasper meditations for supporting change—for me, it is my go-to practice for "ease and flow" that supports my heart choice to just let it go and not worry. I draw great inner strength from the energetic integrity in my heart. Again, it is all about the synergy of the combination that lifts the vibration of our physical, emotional, mental, and spiritual bodies, and the specific affirmations are an integral component of the synergy of this meditation practice. The affirmations allow and facilitate change in ways that continually surprise and delight me—the words remain unchanged each time, but the results are as different as I am each time I change and grow, and then return to this inspired red jasper affirmation practice.

- Please sit in your comfortable meditation position.

- Place four drops of your combined Gentian and Sturt Desert Rose flower essences and red jasper crystal essence under the tongue, anoint your red jasper with a drop of jasmine essential oil and inhale a few drops of jasmine from a tissue or handkerchief while holding your stone in lightly cupped hands.

- Settle into the position, close your eyes, and take a long, slow, deep breath, releasing any tension on the exhale. Repeat with two more breaths.

- Take your awareness behind the eyebrow center. This is the third eye chakra. The color is deep indigo or purple. See yourself sitting in the middle of this space—the one in the middle who intuitively knows.

- Breathe.

- Take your awareness to the crown above you. See it layered with the petals of a closed lotus flower and imagine those petals unfolding, opening to pure positive energy and the infinite field of possibilities.

- Allow the pure white light to illuminate and enliven the deep indigo purple of this space. Feel the energy flood in and cascade through the physical body.

- Breathe.

- Repeat this statement to yourself. *All is clear and simple.*

- Breathe.

- Take your awareness to just below the navel center. This is the sacral chakra. The color is a rich orange. See the pelvic area as a golden bowl filled with the vibrant orange waters of creativity. You sit in the middle on a giant lotus leaf, perfectly balanced, fully supported.

- Breathe.

- No matter which way you choose to move, the liquid always returns to balance with you perfectly supported in the middle.

- Breathe.

- Repeat this statement to yourself. *I am gifted ease and flow.*

- Breathe.

- Take your awareness to the chest center. This is the heart chakra—the middle chakra, that which bridges the upper three and lower three. The color is vibrant emerald or forest green. See yourself in the middle on a vibrant pink and white lotus flower atop a green lotus leaf. You are seated in your heart, the center of unconditional love.

- Breathe.

- See the heart center flooded with Divine energy from above as life-force energy rises to meet it from below. You are supported in Love from above and below.

- Repeat this statement to yourself. *I am in integrity when I choose and act from the heart.*

- Breathe.

- This powerful energy from your heart center floods down your arms and out through your hands to touch the world. You are fully supported and in your power as you choose to act from your heart.

- Repeat the full affirmation, feeling Spirit, or your innate Divinity, Higher Self, or beautiful Inner Being speaking to you. *All is clear and simple, and you are gifted ease and flow. You are in integrity when you choose and act from your beautiful heart. You are energy being human.*

- Breathe. Remain in this space, feeling this space, for as long as it feels comfortable, or as long as your schedule allows.

- When you are ready, take a deep breath and bring your awareness back to the crown. See the petals of the lotus flower closing once again—yours to open at will, and close at will.

- Take another long, slow breath.

- Bring your awareness back into the body. Wiggle your toes and fingers, gently move your hands and your head, and open your eyes to bring your awareness fully back into this moment.

- Express gratitude for All That Is and the gift of grace … and be aware that your Source is even more grateful for all that you are, and all that you are becoming. And so It is.

Meditation to Connect with Archangel Raguel, Higher Self, and Spirit Guides and Teachers

This simple meditation is often favored by those who already enjoy working with archangels, Spirit, guides, or teachers, but please remember that they are all aspects of our innate Divinity or essence. Whether you wish to connect with the energy of Archangel Raguel for motivation and support, or to find harmony in a situation or the harmonious resolution available from broader perspective, or whether you wish to connect to your own Inner Being, the synergy of the red jasper combination will powerfully support your heartfelt intention to be present in the moment and to be open to allow that which is there for you to flow to you.

- Please sit in your comfortable meditation position.

- Place four drops of your combined Gentian and Sturt Desert Rose flower essences and red jasper crystal essence under the tongue, anoint your red jasper with a drop of jasmine essential oil, inhale a few drops of the exotically inspirational jasmine oil from a tissue or handkerchief and throughout the meditation if you feel inspired to do so, and hold your stone in lightly cupped hands.

- Settle into the position, close your eyes, and take a long, slow, deep breath, releasing any tension on the exhale. Repeat with two more breaths.

- Feeling relaxed, still, and present to the moment, please state your intentions. *I am present for all that is here for me. I am listening, and you are welcome.*

- Breathe and release any tension with a long exhalation.

- The soft sound of the breath mirrors the tranquil space of silence where inner peace and harmony are found. Feel the breath, hear the breath, and allow for any awareness of connection that follows.

- Feel deep appreciation and gratitude for this time of connection to a Divine messenger, teacher, or aspect of Oneness, and come out of the meditation whenever you are ready.

Please know that no matter what you feel or do not feel during the meditation, any question you have asked has been answered, any clarity you are seeking has been forthcoming, and any connection you desired has been facilitated by the synergy of the high vibrational combination of red jasper crystal, jasmine essential oil, and red jasper, Gentian, and Sturt Desert Rose essence blend, and Archangel Raguel. Your conscious awareness of clarity, simplicity, and ease and flow when you choose to think, speak, and act in integrity with that which you are, have been awakened and heightened. If this is not a familiar practice for you, please be reassured that enhanced connection is always facilitated and clarity and answers always provided. Sometimes guidance will flow into your consciousness during the practice, sometimes you will be inspired to pick up a particular book, or turn onto a certain radio or television channel, or bump into someone as you go about your day. The answers and clarity always flow, but we do not always get to micromanage how they come to us. Indeed, trusting in our inherent guidance will always deliver that which we seek in the quickest, most direct, and life-enhancing way . . . we just need to trust.

Remember, it is in the smallest of moments that miracles happen and the integrity, harmony, and empowerment of Raguel and associated teachers and guides, including your Higher Self, facilitated through the synergy of the nurturing red jasper combination is indeed inspired.

Moonstone

TRADITIONAL CHAKRA ASSOCIATION
Third Eye (6th) • Crown (7th)

MAIN APPLICATIONS
Calm • Balance • Power • Connection

SYNERGISTIC COMBINATION
Crystal: Moonstone
Essential Oil: Carrot Seed
Flower Essences: Impatiens and Fringed Violet
Archangel: Metatron

Moonstone connects with the powerful Divine Feminine, the moon, and yin energy. Commonly known as a "stone of new beginnings," captivating moonstone is a stone of rebirth that enhances awareness of the natural cycles and stages of life, and the inevitability of change.

However, moonstone's most powerful property is its calming effect on emotions and the gentle way in which it brings forth the emotions; it calms and soothes that which is out of balance. Moonstone is highly effective for those who feel emotionally overwhelmed or feel like a victim of their emotions—its action is gentle but no less powerful than others that are more confronting or highlighting.

This stone is highly personal to the wearer or user—it neither adds nor detracts, but brings to light what is. The unconscious becomes conscious, our intuition heightened as we become aware that intuition is Spirit speaking with us—we become more aware and accepting of All That Is and able to act from a powerful place of understanding and empathy. Moonstone is an excellent meditation aid, facilitating reflection of what is, as well as a gentle exploration and awareness of self. It was traditionally used to promote inspiration and psychic ability, and has long been held sacred in India.

Moonstone's healing comes from its stimulation of the tiny pinecone shaped pineal gland in the midbrain, which links to the hypothalamus and likewise connects the endocrine and nervous systems. The pineal gland is a gateway to time, space, archangels, and teachers; it influences sexual development and regulates our innate body clock. Moonstone facilitates the alignment and balance of the body's cycles with that of the Earth and the Universe.

Although regarded as helpful for women and teenagers, moonstone is also a powerful aid to men and boys needing to balance their emotions. It can be the perfect facilitator for the overly macho male or the overly aggressive female of any age. Moonstone calms hyperactive children.

This is a stone that encourages balance and inner growth and inner strength; it balances the male and the female energies, the yin and yang. It balances the emotions and emotional reactions to situations or ingrained triggers—unhelpful reactions are replaced with considered responses. Moonstone supports release of entrenched negative beliefs: negative energy is undone, dissolved, and transmuted for the higher good. Our willing participation can facilitate lasting change.

Revitalize this stone of balance and rebirth by placing it in the light of the full moon.

How Moonstone Facilitates Well-Being

- Moonstone awakens us to the synchronicities of life—we begin to understand actions that, mentally, seem sudden and irrational; there are no coincidences.

- It soothes and calms emotional distress and instability; it is helpful for shock and enhances a calm response where previously there may have been overreaction.

- Yin and yang are balanced—calming and balancing us emotionally and mentally. Moonstone is highly useful for calming hyperactive children.

- Place moonstone on the solar plexus to draw off old negative emotional patterning—it is highly effective for those emotional problems that manifest as upper digestive tract disorders, such as bloating.

. . . .

This is such an interesting synergistic combination, and definitely a favorite—but truth be told, this was the most troublesome for me as I allowed my thinking brain to try to manipulate my emotional and heart brains. What another perfect analogy for needing this synergistic combination—I was thrown completely off-kilter as I railed and argued against my intuitive guidance and resonance testing!

Questioning guidance is healthy; we all need checks and balances as we go through life. Deliberately connecting into Spirit for guidance and then stubbornly arguing with the guidance provided can be a pretty funny or a pretty painful experience, as we, in effect argue with ourselves, our own Inner Being, our Higher Self, and Spirit—it's an argument we cannot win, but one that can cause us incredible stress.

However, in the end I do always honor the guidance I receive. Sometimes it may take a little time as I seek to make sense of it, but I eventually come to acceptance and gratitude for that which I may have been stubbornly holding out against. The very first person who held a carrot seed–anointed moonstone while receiving a quick seated Reiki treatment reported such a powerful positive response that I no longer doubted the magic of these two gifts working synergistically together. She was not interested in crystal therapy, had tried it in the past but "didn't get it," and so her request to take the stone after the treatment stimulated a warm flow of awareness through me.

I stopped the struggle and mental anguish and decided to immerse myself in the synergistic combination ... and listen while the rest of the synergistic combination was "unearthed" to me: it is Earth to Sky perfectly reflected. There were many *ah-ha* moments as I explored, immersed, and integrated, but the most joyful was awareness that came from a broader view of the complete combination. For example, this powerfully gentle white stone resonates synergistically with an orange essential oil and violet/purple flowers with tiny green centers, which reflect three main chakras—third eye, heart, and sacral (intuitive, heart, and emotional centers)—and the pure white of that which contains all, All That Is. How perfect for facilitating wellness and well-being.

Essential Oils, Flower Essences, and Spirit Connection

Moonstone benefits our being very well on its own, but those benefits are expanded to bring unimagined versatility when used in combination. The synergy of the following combinations encourages a sense of gentle renewal, empowerment, and wonder that will calm and excite you as you go forward.

Essential Oils

The highest resonance is between moonstone and carrot seed essential oil. Traditionally, moonstone is used with the third eye and crown chakras but this power combination works effectively and synergistically to harmonize the whole being whether the crystal is placed on the body, held, worn, carried in the pocket, or placed nearby.

Carrot seed (*Daucus carota*) essential oil is distilled from the seeds of the wild carrot and there is also oil in the whole plant—this is not to be confused with carrot oil which is often base oil infused with macerated plant material or solvent extracted. Carrot seed essential oil has a soft, warm, dry, earthy, sweet aroma with the familiar smell of carrot, and is probably one of the most underestimated and overlooked essential oils in aromatherapy. Popular for cleansing, toning, purifying and healing the skin, rejuvenating elasticity, and fading "age spots" or "liver spots," this wonderful essential oil brings so much more to every level of our being.

Just as it detoxifies, clears, and enhances the tone of the skin, carrot seed also detoxifies, clears, purifies, and balances the subtle bodies and the chakras. This oil has been highlighted as particularly helpful when balancing the sacral, solar plexus, heart, and third eye chakras. Carrot seed essential oil is uplifting, soothing, and balancing.

This oil's action is a wonderful example of the outer reflecting the inner, as our inner life, that which we so often keep hidden, is reflected through our eyes and the outer skin. Carrot seed helps purify and open our third eye so we are in touch with our intuition, and as we hear the voice of Spirit we are able to see things from a broader perspective. Changing our perspective from that of ego to that of broader perspective will always soothe the emotional body; soothing the emotional body, settling and balancing our emotions, will always be reflected in our eyes and skin, which in turn will be soothed. Stress is relieved, we are soothed, and we are gently helped with new insights and perspective. We are connected on every level—body, mind, and spirit. Every layer contributes to the whole, and we are so much more than our component parts.

On the emotional barometer, carrot seed essential oil aligns with the emotional body, helping us move from feeling emotionally overwhelmed to feeling emotionally balanced.

....

Creating this synergistic combination was a bumpy ride as my mental thoughts offered up good reasons why I had it wrong when it came to the essential oil component. This was always the first step in the creative process as it was the essential oil that I would use to clear the crystal to support the next stage of creating the synergistic combination.

Carrot seed essential oil just did not make sense to me, yet the guidance was consistent and constant and the resonance between moonstone and carrot seed essential oil was powerful, unmatched, undeniable, and unequivocal; yet my head kept worrying that the oil color might stain and the earthy aroma did not have that uplifting sensual tone that so many are drawn to. *What if they don't like the aroma? Moonstone is a much-loved stone...putting carrot seed with it just sounds silly.* And then I would swing into fear and self-doubt with *No one will believe this. Are you sure, what about...* and so began another cycle of retrying of the resonance, doggedly trying to find something better. I just could not get my head around the fact that the essential oil was so earthy and the stone was so delicate.

So, if the moonstone synergistic combination gives you pause and variations spring to mind, please know that in the end, it is perfect. It brings a feeling of Oneness, and appreciation of the power that comes from such connection. It is earthy, grounding, and stabilizing, and yet uplifting, expansive, and wondrous. We are, indeed, gifted by the synergy of the moonstone combination.

Flower Essences

The highest resonance is between moonstone and Impatiens Bach Flower and Fringed Violet Australian Bush Flower Essences.

Impatiens Bach Flower Essence relates to the qualities of patience, compassion, empathy, and gentleness. The negative Impatiens type is impatient, irritable, stressed, quick-thinking, intolerant of others, and would much prefer to work alone because others cannot keep up; their frustration and impatience often causes them to be angry, but the anger usually flares and passes quite quickly. This is an excellent, fast-acting remedy for children prone to squabbles and temper tantrums.

This is the remedy for the quick-minded, fast-talking, and fast-acting—those who grasp new ideas and concepts quickly, and are smart, efficient and intuitive in anything they choose to do. The Impatiens type is highly capable. The outcome of the irritation and impatience of this type often manifests as tension in the physical body and can range from tension pain to irritation of the skin and digestion from emotional upsets.

The potential Impatiens transformation brings one back into balance so that the positive qualities of great gentleness, tolerance, empathy, and sympathy toward others are evident. Dr. Bach is reputed to have used Impatiens to counter a rash that would suddenly appear when he became irritated and impatient with others less gifted than he and slower to understand. A single dose of this fast-acting remedy would reportedly restore his gentle manner and good humor. Dr. Bach exemplifies the positive Impatiens type: highly capable, clever, decisive, and intuitive, but displays genuine tolerance, compassion, empathy, and angelic patience of those around them as they think with their hearts.

Fringed Violet bursts forth for just one single morning to display its purple beauty with fringed hairs framing the petals like an aura. Its radiating beauty is such a fitting analogy as one of the leading applications for Fringed Violet Australian Bush Flower Essence: restoration of an aura that has been damaged through shock or trauma. This remedy protects us from being thrown off-kilter, or emotionally off balance by external influences.

We live in a world of vibration in a vibratory universe; the cells in our body constantly vibrate as do the particles within each cell, and when the aura is negatively impacted by any external influence, situation, person, or event, that optimal vibration is affected and can, in turn, present as a variety of physical and emotional imbalances and irritations.

This remedy is for those times we feel drained by external energies, especially the harmful negative energies of others. There are times when each of us, particularly those of us who are very sensitive, can be unaware that we are absorbing the negative emotion, emotional imbalance, pain, and upsets of others, or indeed, we are under intentional psychic attack—either way, we are in need of psychic protection.

Fringed Violet helps protect us and restore the aura that may have been negatively impacted by any range of external influences, which then manifests in physical, mental, and emotional dysfunction. Fringed Violet helps reintegrate the physical and subtle bodies and balance us very much in the here and now; we become very present.

Archangels

The highest resonance is between moonstone and Archangel Metatron.

Archangel Metatron is known as the Angel of the Presence or the Angel of Life, and one of the two archangels to have lived in physical: Metatron was the Biblical scribe and wise man, Enoch, who was said to walk with God. Metatron is regarded as the youngest and the tallest archangel, and for me is the perfect analogy of that energy which links Mother Earth to Spirit and All That Is.

Metatron is a powerful guide as we commence a spiritual journey, and then brings ongoing spiritual understanding and awareness as we proceed on our chosen path. He supports our ability to be present to the moment, accepting of that which we cannot control, and to be in appreciation of the moment. We feel balanced; we can see both sides of a situation, take a broader view, and choose, decide, and act with appreciation and respect for all. We feel calm, grounded, and motivated, and choose with self-respect, self-discipline, and self-awareness—we respond to a situation rather than reacting without care or thought of self and those around us.

Metatron brought us the healing and time-warping Merkaba, or Metatron's Cube, and teachings of sacred geometry. He helps balance mental and emotional imbalances in children, such as hyperactivity and ADHD, and he actively assists those who continue to come forth with heightened awareness and struggle with a sense of limitation and restriction in physical.

Metatron enhances meditation and facilitates an ability to be still; we feel balanced, purified, and cleansed by the ever-constant and consistent energy that washes through us, restoring mental and emotional balance. Self-worth and self-belief are restored, and there is awareness of the infinite joy, love, and abundance available to each and every one of us. We feel empowered, calm, and balanced.

....

When I first began synergistically combining the gifts from Mother Earth and Spirit, Metatron was one of the archangels that I called in to "prove" that this stuff I was embracing and integrating was real.

A very young hyperactive friend was struggling, mentally and emotionally, and the parents were likewise struggling and concerned. I called in Metatron to prove his mettle, so to speak, and asked that he watch over, guide, and facilitate an easier passage for this young friend who I held dear; I did not seek to interfere or control any outcome, simply guidance to ease the transitions.

Needless to say, within a very short time my "proof" was forthcoming and my overwhelming gratitude heartfelt; I received word that this young friend seemed to have turned the tide and was doing well. I am continually appreciative of Metatron's ongoing support of my young friend, and I am in continual wonder of the gifts I receive from the synergy of the moonstone combination.

Meditation Practices

By choosing to quiet the mind with the moonstone synergistic combination we open up to the power of softness and our innate perfect balance, as the physical integrates with the spiritual, through the mental and emotional bodies. We embrace a sense of wonder at the innate order, balance, and perfection in it all as we feel equally calm and excited about what is to come. The infinite field of possibilities and potentialities is there for each of us. There is an elusive richness to a life that is regularly refreshed and aligned by quiet time alone in contemplation.

For the following meditations, please have at hand your crystal, essential oil, and crystal and flower essences. The crystal essence and combined flower essences may be taken in a single blend, or used separately, as is most convenient to you. The essential oil may certainly be vaporized in an oil burner to fill the meditation space, but as this is not always doable or convenient in some locations, please be assured that a few drops of essential oil on a tissue or handkerchief will serve you well at any time and in any location—whether meditating at home or in the moonlight, or simply connecting in while feeling surrounded by chaos.

Sit in whatever way is comfortable for you—if seated in a chair, have your feet flat on the floor with no shoes. Ensure your back is straight by gently lifting your heart center. Relax your shoulders. Lengthen the back of the neck by slightly tilting the chin downward.

Take a couple of breaths and bring yourself to a place of quiet appreciation of this time that you are gifting you.

Meditation to Connect with the Moonstone Synergy

Many will regard this as the least complicated and most "earthy" of the three moonstone meditations. In this meditation, we connect to the high vibrational energy that is created by the specific combination of these gifts from Mother Earth: moonstone stone, carrot seed essential oil, and a blend of moonstone, Impatiens, and Fringed Violet essences. As always, it is all about the synergy of the combination. I use this meditation whenever I feel in need of the balance, clarity, and gentle strength that inevitably follow as I am calmed and uplifted. To connect with the moonstone synergy, you will need:

Moonstone crystal

Carrot seed essential oil

Impatiens and Fringed Violet flower essences

Moonstone crystal essence

- Place four drops of the combined Impatiens and Fringed Violet flower essences and moonstone crystal essence under your tongue. Take a breath.

- Anoint the moonstone with a drop of carrot seed essential oil. Inhale the sweet earthy aroma as you gently rub the oil into the stone, breathing slowly and deeply.

- Cup the moonstone lightly in your hands—the fingertips of the right hand gently touch the base of the left palm—and rest your hands comfortably in your lap. Take a deep breath, softly close your eyes, and release any tightness with the exhalation.

- Feel the energy of the moonstone as it fills your cupped hands—for example, it may feel tingling, effervescent, light, heavy, or like your hands are suctioned together or they may expand apart during the session—there is no right way it should feel, and how it feels is right for you.

- Feel or imagine the energy moving up through your arms, through to your gentle heart center, and radiating out to fill your being in whatever way feels right for you.

- Know that the synergy of the combination will equally calm, stimulate, heal, or enhance that which needs attention at this time.

- You may see the soft glow of the moonstone behind the closed eyes—maybe with flashes of color, maybe an expansive white glow, or color that fades in and out, as the energy of the moonstone combination connects with, balances, strengthens and expands various energy centers.

- You are calm, balanced, and powerful in this space. Feel gratitude for any understanding that may flow to you and let it go. Trust that any insight, inspiration, or awareness has settled into your being and will be with you, guiding and balancing you, when you come out of the meditation.

- Feel the energy. Be in wonder of the synergy of these combined gifts from Mother Earth. Luxuriate in the calm inner strength of connection, and allow it to nourish you and sustain you. Remain within that expansive grounded space for as long as you wish.

Meditation on the Essence of the Moonstone Combination (with Affirmations)

Of the three moonstone meditations, this one will most powerfully support change as we choose from the heart to release the struggle within and find calm. The inner power that we can draw from balance will never disappoint. Again, it is all about the synergy of the combination that lifts the vibration of our physical, emotional, mental, and spiritual bodies, and the specific affirmations are an integral component of the synergy of this meditation practice. The affirmations allow and facilitate change in ways that continually surprise and delight me—the words remain unchanged each time, but the results are as different as I am each time I change and grow, and then return to this inspired moonstone affirmation practice.

- Please sit in your comfortable meditation position.

- Place four drops of your combined Impatiens and Fringed Violet flower essences and moonstone crystal essence under the tongue, anoint your moonstone with a drop of carrot seed essential oil and inhale a few drops of carrot seed from a tissue or handkerchief while holding your stone in lightly cupped hands.

- Settle into the position, close your eyes, and take a long, slow, deep breath, releasing any tension on the exhale. Repeat with two more breaths.

- Take your awareness behind the eyebrow center. This is the third eye chakra. The color is deep indigo or purple. See yourself sitting in the middle of this space—the one in the middle who intuitively knows.

- Breathe.

- Take your awareness to the crown above you. See it layered with the petals of a closed lotus flower and imagine those petals unfolding, opening to pure positive energy and the infinite field of possibilities.

- Allow the pure white light to illuminate and enliven the deep indigo purple of this space. Feel the energy flood in and cascade through the physical body.

- Breathe.

- Repeat this statement to yourself. *I feel equally calm and excited about what is to come.*

- Breathe.

- Take your awareness to just below the navel center. This is the sacral chakra. The color is a rich orange. See the pelvic area as a golden bowl filled with the vibrant orange waters of creativity. You sit in the middle on a giant lotus leaf, perfectly balanced, fully supported.

- Breathe.

- No matter which way you choose to move, the liquid always returns to balance with you perfectly supported in the middle.

- Breathe.

- Repeat this statement to yourself. *I find calm and balance in any storm.*

- Breathe.

- Take your awareness to the chest center. This is the heart chakra—the middle chakra, that which bridges the upper three and lower three. The color is vibrant emerald or forest green. See yourself in the middle on a vibrant pink and white lotus flower atop a green lotus leaf. You are seated in your heart, the center of unconditional love.

- Breathe.

- See the heart center flooded with Divine energy from above as life-force energy rises to meet it from below. You are supported in Love from above and below.

- Repeat this statement to yourself. *My power comes from a soft gentle center.*

- Breathe.

- This powerful energy from your heart center floods down your arms and out through your hands to touch the world. You are fully supported and in your power as you choose to act from your heart.

- Repeat the full affirmation, feeling Spirit, or your innate Divinity, Higher Self, or beautiful Inner Being speaking to you. *Be equally calm and excited about what is to come, and find calm and balance in any storm. Your power comes from a soft gentle center. You are energy being human.*

- Breathe. Remain in this space, feeling this space, for as long as it feels comfortable, or as long as your schedule allows.

- When you are ready, take a deep breath and bring your awareness back to the crown. See the petals of the lotus flower closing once again—yours to open at will, and close at will.

- Take another long, slow breath.

- Bring your awareness back into the body. Wiggle your toes and fingers, gently move your hands and your head, and open your eyes to bring your awareness fully back into this moment.

- Express gratitude for All That Is and the gift of grace … and be aware that your Source is even more grateful for all that you are, and all that you are becoming. And so It is.

Meditation to Connect with Archangel Metatron, Higher Self, and Spirit Guides and Teachers

This simple meditation is often favored by those who already enjoy working with archangels, Spirit, guides, or teachers, but please remember that they are all aspects of our innate Divinity or essence. Whether you wish to connect with the energy of Archangel Metatron for an enhanced sense of connection, strength, stillness and presence, or whether you wish to connect to your own Inner Being, the synergy of the moonstone combination will powerfully support your heartfelt intention to be present in the moment and to be open to allow that which is there for you to flow to you.

- Please sit in your comfortable meditation position.

- Place four drops of your combined Impatiens and Fringed Violet flower essences and moonstone crystal essence under the tongue, anoint your moonstone with a drop of carrot seed essential oil, inhale a few drops of the balanced sweet earthy aroma of carrot seed oil from a tissue or handkerchief and throughout the meditation if you feel inspired to do so, and hold your stone in lightly cupped hands.

- Settle into the position, close your eyes, and take a long, slow, deep breath, releasing any tension on the exhale. Repeat with two more breaths.

- Feeling relaxed, still, and present to the moment, please state your intentions. *I am present for all that is here for me. I am listening, and you are welcome.*

- Breathe and release any tension with a long exhalation.

- The soft sound of the breath mirrors the tranquil space of silence where inner peace and harmony are found. Feel the breath, hear the breath, and allow for any awareness of connection that follows.

- Feel deep appreciation and gratitude for this time of connection to a Divine messenger, teacher, or aspect of Oneness, and come out of the meditation whenever you are ready.

Please know that no matter what you feel or do not feel during the meditation, any question you have asked has been answered, any clarity you are seeking has been forthcoming, and any connection you desired has been facilitated by the synergy of the high vibrational combination of moonstone crystal, carrot seed essential oil, and the moonstone, Impatiens, and Fringed Violet essence blend, and Archangel Metatron. Your conscious awareness and sense of the innate calm, balance, power, and connection that is ever-present and constant in the stillness within have been awakened and heightened. If this is not a familiar practice for you, please be reassured that enhanced connection is always facilitated and clarity and answers always provided. Sometimes guidance will flow into your consciousness during the practice, sometimes you will be inspired to pick up a particular book, or turn onto a certain radio or television channel, or bump into someone as you go about your day. The answers and clarity always flow, but we do not always get to micromanage how they come to us. Indeed, trusting in our inherent guidance will always deliver that which we seek in the quickest, most direct, and life-enhancing way... we just need to trust.

Remember, it is in the smallest of moments that miracles happen and the presence and balance of Metatron and associated teachers and guides, including your Higher Self, facilitated through the synergy of the moonstone combination is indeed inspired.

Quartz, Clear

TRADITIONAL CHAKRA ASSOCIATION
Higher Crown (8th) • All Chakras

MAIN APPLICATIONS
Assertiveness • Choice without Fear
Embracing All We Are • Being All We Are

SYNERGISTIC COMBINATION
Crystal: Clear Quartz
Essential Oil: Neroli and Frankincense
Flower Essences: Centaury and Green Spider Orchid
Archangel: Michael

Clear quartz crystal, also called rock crystal, was originally found by the ancients in the frozen mountains of the high Alps—they believed it to be a miraculous ice crystal that could never melt.

Quartz is the most powerful healer and energy amplifier that we are gifted by Mother Earth—it absorbs, stores, releases, and regulates energy. Kirlian photography has demonstrated how holding a piece of quartz doubles our biomagnetic field; it is also clearly demonstrated by enhanced muscle testing.

Quartz generates electromagnetic energy and will dispel static electricity and protect against radiation.

This dynamic stone amplifies the vibration of other crystals and is a powerful stone to use at any time—in crystal therapy it is the go-to stone, particularly if there is a lack of clarity as to the best stone to use, or when stones specific for the symptoms are unavailable.

Various shapes are favored for some techniques: in healing work, the shape called a "point" or "double point" is the optimal to use; spheres have long been used for scrying to predict the future, and spheres and eggs are ideal for meditation. However, if you have a favorite stone or shape that feels right in your hand, then please continue to enjoy that. When we embrace these gifts from the Earth, nothing matters more than how we feel with the stone—that is always the highest guidance.

Quartz crystal resonates most closely to us as humans and whether used for meditation or simply kept close, it helps one to know one's true self. Spiritually, clear quartz raises our energy to the highest possible level—it contains every color possible and therefore works on all levels. The powerfully constant vibration resonated by quartz, which has proved so technologically useful for all manner of mechanisms, is no less harmonizing for the human mechanism. There is a great sense of freedom in such harmony.

Clear quartz will dissolve karmic cords and seeds that we are prepared to release—we lovingly and willingly release them to be undone, dissolved and transmuted into pure positive energy for redistribution for the highest good.

Each of us has our own innate willpower and freedom to choose, and we can choose to not be open to receiving the harmonizing energy of quartz, or any other stone, at any time—but sadly, some who do choose to walk a more connected path are unaware that fear is preventing them from receiving the gifts that are there for each of us. Releasing and dissolving fear offers such freedom. Psychic awareness is enhanced and we become attuned to our life or spiritual purpose.

How Clear Quartz Facilitates Well-Being

- Clear quartz connects the physical with that which the Buddhists call Mind, or All That Is.

- Its ability to align and attune vibration makes clear quartz highly useful for programming with our intent.

- It is a powerful aid to meditation as distractions are filtered out.

- Spiritually, it raises energy to the highest possible and has the ability to undo and dissolve karmic threads and seeds.

- Quartz is an excellent aid to focusing attention and unblocking the memory.

. . . .

This clear quartz synergistic combination was one of my first synergistic combinations using the various gifts from the Earth, and after feeling the stone's powerful resonance with the oils and the equally powerful clear guidance that identified the complete combination, I decided to immerse myself in the synergy of the combination and willingly release the fears and entrenched negative beliefs that were rooted firmly in the past.

There were a number of releases triggered by memory flashes, feelings, and life encounters as the process unfolded; each time I honored the moment and once again released negative cords and hooks that were causing limitation and preventing me from being all that I chose to be. As I immersed myself in the process, so the concurrent processes of me evolving and integrating, and creating the synergistic combinations and practices began.

The synergy of the clear quartz combination and practices has empowered me to trust that which I have learned and integrated, to walk my talk, and to fearlessly and lovingly share with those who are interested ... and my synergistically prepared flat stone provides powerful and constant support whenever I feel I need it.

Essential Oils, Flower Essences, and Spirit Connection

Clear quartz is a powerful stone that resonates with all levels of our being, of that there is no doubt. However, to combine the brilliance of the master crystal with the following gifts is to unleash the synergy that transforms and empowers in ways that will surprise and delight you, and encourage you to fearlessly be all that you choose to be.

Essential Oils

Neroli essential oil has been cited by other practitioners as resonating with clear quartz. However, the highest and equally powerful resonance is between clear quartz and both neroli and frankincense essential oils. Traditionally, clear quartz is used with the higher crown chakra and, indeed, all the chakras. This power combination greatly enhances the connection, working effectively and synergistically to harmonize the whole being whether the crystal is placed on the body, held, worn, carried in the pocket, or placed nearby.

There should be no surprise that one of the oils that fully harmonizes with the purity, vibrancy, clarity, and radiance of clear quartz is that extracted from the pure white blossoms of the bitter orange (*Citrus aurantium*): neroli.

The delicate pale yellow neroli oil, whether extracted by steam distillation or the time-consuming enfleurage method, is one of the more expensive to produce. However, this precious oil is profoundly calming to the physical body and will purify any space or bring immediate tranquility and reassuring reconnection when inhaled from a tissue or handkerchief.

This refreshing, relaxing, calming, and uplifting oil will calm a charged emotional state, uplift from anxiety and depression, and help with confusion, poor concentration, apathy, despair, despondency, lethargy, fear, irritability, jealousy, panic, shock, and restlessness ... to mention but a few of its applications.

On the emotional barometer, neroli aligns with the spiritual body transforming the negative feelings of no choice into an expansive awareness of the unlimited choices that are available to us. This delightful fragrance bridges the subtle bodies, bringing renewal and alignment that encourages awareness of consequences, and considered and empowered choices. We are empowered to change, and that is no small feat!

Frankincense (*Boswellia carterii* and *B. sacra*) is produced from the gum of the Boswellia tree in hot dry areas of the Mediterranean and Middle East.

This spicy intoxicating oil was prized by the ancient Egyptians five thousand years ago, highlighted in Biblical stories of Jesus, and highly valued as an important part of ceremonial incenses.

Apart from its wonderful cleansing, pain-relieving, healing, and protective properties for physical treatments, frankincense will stimulate and uplift, refresh and rejuvenate, or calm and sedate as required. It heals on all levels: physically, emotionally, and mentally.

On the emotional barometer, frankincense connects with the spiritual body to shift our spirit from feeling vulnerable to feeling protected. The properties of this wonderfully woody, sweet, spicy fragrance attune to the subtle bodies and open us to Higher Self. Used to support meditation, frankincense will help to slow the breath and facilitate a quiet calm journey as one explores that which is within. This wonderful oil brings balance, stability, and protection to the heart that is vulnerable; our innate peaceful warrior is awakened, and we become aware and trusting of our inherent strength and inner protector and champion.

You may choose to use either neroli or frankincense with clear quartz . . . or you may feel drawn to use both, as I so often do. A drop or two each of neroli and frankincense on a tissue to inhale throughout the day, together with the feel of a quartz stone in your pocket prepared with the oils brings a powerful feeling of connection and support.

Flower Essences

The highest resonance is between clear quartz and Centaury Bach Flower and Green Spider Orchid Australian Bush Flower Essences.

Centaury is the Bach Flower Essence for those who are oversensitive and allow themselves to be imposed upon—they may have difficulty saying "no" and allow themselves to be exploited. Centaury is the "doormat remedy" for those who often feel drained from the strain of constantly doing for others, and some may even appear timid or lack individuality as they become more like the stronger personality.

There is low self-esteem and poor self-will as we have forgotten, or temporarily lost touch with, our innate life-force gift of self-will and self-determination. In service of others, we have lost sight of our own sense of purpose and fulfillment.

The potential Centaury transformation is one of self-determination, self-realization, and self-responsibility to draw the line—there is quiet power in knowing where our line in the sand is. No longer the gofer in any group or situation, our subservience is replaced by discernment and discrimination as we *choose* whether to withhold or serve. Our innate sensitivity and sense of service and devotion become strengths of great virtue; we remain true to ourselves and feel strong in our individuality as we choose to follow our life purpose.

Indeed, many consider the negative Centaury state affects the most sensitive among us: when we commence a path of higher awareness, we can often swing wildly out of balance with disharmony pain and hurt, until we adjust and don't allow ourselves to be the victim of those who wish us harm, or to divert or unduly influence us. The positive Centaury is empowered by quiet inner strength and self-realization to deliberately allow the Divine life force to flow to them, through them, and out from them to serve the highest good in support of whatever life purpose they choose.

The Green Spider Orchid Australian Bush Flower Essence is particularly helpful for those of us who have chosen a spiritual path and for those times when we need acceptance or feel fragile mentally, emotionally, or spiritually. This remedy supports and realigns disharmony in our higher consciousness and helps to rebalance our increased sensitivity to others and external environments.

It is the remedy for attunement and higher learning that brings deeper philosophical, spiritual, and telepathic insight. Karmic cords from past lives that hold us back or present as negative core beliefs or entrenched negative patterns or nightmares can be released, and so this essence further supports our intention to willingly and lovingly release that which no longer serves us well.

The positive Green Spider Orchid transformation brings attunement and enhanced psychic awareness and spiritual connection. We learn to discern and discriminate when to share our spiritual beliefs and experiences, and when to assimilate and integrate that which we have come to know. We no longer place ourselves in that disempowered place of feeling a need to defend that which we are and that which we choose to be. We silently hold the space with our inner knowing, no longer needing to share with the detractors as there is no desire to convince or change another. We allow all to unfold as we know it will and in a way that serves the highest good—the highest good of all concerned, including us.

Archangels

The highest resonance is between clear quartz and Archangel Michael.

Archangel Michael is a leader among the archangels, and his powerful energy is easily felt by those wanting to connect. He is one of the four archangels who particularly facilitate healing: Michael, Raphael, Uriel, and Haniel.

Michael gifts us fearlessness as fear and negativity, willingly released, are dissolved and undone. His classically depicted sword of light represents his purpose to cut the bonds of fear propagated by the negative ego mind; he will slay the ego dragon inside that limits us fulfilling our potential.

The supreme protector, Michael protects and shields all areas of our being but, as always, free will is paramount: we ask; we listen or feel for intuition or gut instinct; we choose to act. Higher guidance is often felt through our Hara (sacral chakra), or "feeling brain." Michael powerfully supports and guides our life purpose; he motivates, protects, supports, and empowers change; he enhances self-esteem, self-worth, self-responsibility, and self-realization, while bringing focus, attention, and logical application to the task at hand. His energy is immediate and powerfully strengthens and supports us on our path. He reminds us of our innate personal power and responsibility to set our own boundaries; we feel strong as Divine life force flows to us and through us.

We understand that thoughts are energy not yet manifested. He brings appreciation of the untapped power of the mind of the individual when it connects to Universal Mind, or All That Is—the Divine lives within us, as us, and is expressed through our humanity. Universal Mind can express through us in ways we have not yet dreamed. We walk our path with grace and embrace all that we are.

....

Nearly twenty years ago I suffered the trauma of an armed holdup while in business. The story and details would serve no purpose here. In the end, physically I was unhurt, but the mental and emotional scars were deep and long-lasting, effectively tucked away in the already burgeoning baggage of "stuff" that so many of us cart around with us.

Despite many life-enhancing changes over the years, I had awareness that what needed to be released had not been released. The shifts and changes took form and direction as I dared to explore and open up to various opportunities—but in the last couple of years, an unfolding of synchronicities presented the opportunity for release that I still hold in wonder.

During a weekend visit to the city, I found myself alone in a backstreet waiting for my husband Gary to collect me. He was late (though he would later reflect on the strange decisions he made that played into this outcome). It was early evening, and I had no phone. All of a sudden, feelings of fear, aloneness, and vulnerability swamped me, and for the first time in my living memory I felt the full heart-pounding hyperventilating confusion of a panic attack. The few who walked by felt potentially threatening. I felt out of control. I could not phone anyone, not even a cab; I could not find anyone I felt comfortable approaching; I felt lost. I could not think straight; the feelings were totally unfamiliar for me.

In that chest-heaving moment, I held on to a nearby signpost for support and demanded, *Michael, if all this stuff is real, settle me now! And give me guidance as to whether Gary is on his way. Do I go or stay?* The cascade of energy that ran through me from top to toe was immediate and warming; the palpitations calmed in an instant; the breath was immediately slow and deep; and all I heard in my monkey-mind was *Stay, he is on his way.* I have never felt so fully supported; I had never previously asked. Of course, all was well, and the unfolding moments of miraculous wonder resulted in a kind stranger calling Gary for me and I heard Gary say, *Just stay, I'm on my way.* He unexpectedly walked around the corner a few moments later. This experience precipitated a wonderful unfolding and growth for me that included the creation of the clear quartz synergistic combination.

Quartz Emergency Fear or Panic Synergistic Combination

There is also a powerful synergy between three forms of quartz—clear, rose, or rutilated quartz—and neroli and frankincense essential oils, Rock Rose Bach and Waratah Australian Bush Flower Essences, and Archangel Michael to effectively treat acute terror, panic, shock, or fright, including calming children after terrifying nightmares. Rock Rose and Waratah flower essences are each noted treatments in these instances, and either treatment can be enhanced by using the complete synergistic combination.

Meditation Practices

By choosing to quiet the mind with the clear quartz synergistic combination we open up to feeling empowered, protected, and fearless, as the physical integrates with the spiritual, through the mental and emotional bodies. We embrace a sense of wonder at the innate balance and perfection in it all, and choose to be all that we are. The infinite field of possibilities and potentialities is there for each of us. There is an elusive richness and strength to a life that is regularly empowered by quiet time alone in contemplation.

For the following meditations, please have at hand your crystal, essential oil, and crystal and flower essences. The crystal essence and combined flower essences may be taken in a single blend, or used separately, as is most convenient to you. The essential oil may certainly be vaporized in an oil burner to fill the meditation space, but as this is not always doable or convenient in some locations, please be assured that a few drops of essential oil on a tissue or handkerchief will serve you well at any time and in any place—whether meditating at home or at the beach, or simply connecting in while waiting in the dentist's waiting room.

Sit in whatever way is comfortable for you—if seated in a chair, have your feet flat on the floor with no shoes. Ensure your back is straight by gently lifting your heart center. Relax your shoulders. Lengthen the back of the neck by slightly tilting the chin downward.

Take a couple of breaths and bring yourself to a place of quiet appreciation of this time that you are gifting you.

Meditation to Connect with the Clear Quartz Synergy

This is the simplest and "earthiest" of the three meditations using a clear quartz combination. In this meditation, we connect to the high vibrational energy that is created by the specific combination of these gifts from Mother Earth: clear quartz stone, frankincense or neroli essential oil, and a blend of clear quartz, Centaury, and Green Spider Orchid essences. As always, it is all about the synergy of the combination. I use this meditation whenever I feel in need of the strength, clarity, and support that inevitably follow as I am uplifted and empowered. To connect with the clear quartz synergy, you will need:

Clear quartz crystal

Neroli and/or frankincense essential oil

Centaury and Green Spider Orchid flower essences

Clear quartz crystal essence

- Place four drops of the combined Centaury and Green Spider Orchid flower essences and clear quartz crystal essence under your tongue. Take a breath.

- Anoint the clear quartz with a drop of neroli and/or frankincense essential oil. (I often use both). Inhale the uplifting and intoxicating fragrance as you gently rub the oil into the stone, breathing slowly and deeply. Take a breath.

- Cup the clear quartz lightly in your hands—the fingertips of the right hand gently touch to the base of the left palm—and rest your hands comfortably in your lap. Take a breath and softly close your eyes.

- Feel the energy of the clear quartz as it fills your cupped hands—for example, it may feel tingling, effervescent, light, heavy, or like your hands are suctioned together or they may expand apart during the session—there is no right way it should feel, and how it feels is right for you.

- Feel or imagine the energy moving up through your arms, through to the heart center, and radiating out to fill your being in whatever way feels right for you.

- Thoughts will come and go; let them. Trust that the synergy of the combination will empower you, cleanse, balance, heal, open, or enhance that which needs attention at this time.

- You may see glittering colors behind the closed eyes—maybe flashes, maybe an expansive mist or swirls of color, or deep color that fades in and out, as the energy of the clear quartz combination connects with various energy centers.

- Feel gratitude for any clarity, motivation, empowerment, or awareness that comes to you and let it go, trusting that it will be there for you when you come out of the meditation.

- Feel the energy. Be in wonder of the synergy of these combined gifts from Mother Earth. Luxuriate in the connection; allow it to fill you, empower, expand, and nourish you, and remain within that expansive grounded space for as long as you wish.

Meditation on the Essence of the Clear Quartz Combination (with Affirmations)

Unquestionably, this is the most powerful of the three clear quartz meditations to support change and a heartfelt decision to let go of everything that prevents us being all that we choose to be. Feeling empowered to choose without fear is life changing. Again, it is all about the synergy of the combination that lifts the vibration of our physical, emotional, mental, and spiritual bodies, and the specific affirmations are an integral component of the synergy of this meditation practice. The affirmations allow and facilitate change in ways that continually surprise and delight me—the words remain unchanged each time, but the results are as different as I am each time I change and grow, and then return to this inspired clear quartz affirmation practice.

- Please sit in your comfortable meditation position.

- Place four drops of your combined Centaury and Green Spider Orchid flower essences and clear quartz crystal essence under the tongue, anoint your clear quartz with a drop of neroli and/or frankincense essential oils and inhale a few drops of neroli and/or frankincense from a tissue or handkerchief while holding your stone in lightly cupped hands.

- Settle into the position, close your eyes, and take a long, slow, deep breath, releasing any tension on the exhale. Repeat with two more breaths.

- Take your awareness behind the eyebrow center. This is the third eye chakra. The color is deep indigo or purple. See yourself sitting in the middle of this space—the one in the middle who intuitively knows.

- Breathe.

- Take your awareness to the crown above you. See it layered with the petals of a closed lotus flower and imagine those petals unfolding, opening to pure positive energy and the infinite field of possibilities.

- Allow the pure white light to illuminate and enliven the deep indigo purple of this space. Feel the energy flood in and cascade through the physical body.

- Breathe.

- Repeat this statement to yourself. *I can be however I choose to be.*

- Breathe.

- Take your awareness to just below the navel center. This is the sacral chakra. The color is a rich orange. See the pelvic area as a golden bowl filled with the vibrant orange waters of creativity. You sit in the middle on a giant lotus leaf, perfectly balanced, fully supported.

- Breathe.

- No matter which way you choose to move, the liquid always returns to balance with you perfectly supported in the middle.

- Breathe.

- Repeat this statement to yourself. *I can be fearless in my choices.*

- Breathe.

- Take your awareness to the chest center. This is the heart chakra—the middle chakra, that which bridges the upper three and lower three. The color is vibrant emerald or forest green. See yourself in the middle on a vibrant pink and white lotus flower atop a green lotus leaf. You are seated in your heart, the center of unconditional love.

- Breathe.

- See the heart center flooded with Divine energy from above as life-force energy rises to meet it from below. You are supported in Love from above and below.

- Repeat this statement to yourself. *I can be all that I choose to be.*

- Breathe.

- This powerful energy from your heart center floods down your arms and out through your hands to touch the world. You are fully supported and in your power as you choose to act from your heart.

- Repeat the full affirmation, feeling Spirit, or your innate Divinity, Higher Self, or beautiful Inner Being speaking to you. *You can be however you choose to be, and fearless in your choices. You can be all that you choose to be. You are energy being human.*

- Breathe. Remain in this space, feeling this space, for as long as it feels comfortable, or as long as your schedule allows.

- When you are ready, take a deep breath and bring your awareness back to the crown. See the petals of the lotus flower closing once again—yours to open at will, and close at will.

- Take another long, slow breath.

- Bring your awareness back into the body. Wiggle your toes and fingers, gently move your hands and your head, and open your eyes to bring your awareness fully back into this moment.

- Express gratitude for All That Is and the gift of grace ... and be aware that your Source is even more grateful for all that you are, and all that you are becoming. And so It is.

Meditation to Connect with Archangel Michael, Higher Self, and Spirit Guides and Teachers

This simple meditation is often favored by those who already enjoy working with archangels, Spirit, guides, or teachers, but please remember that they are all aspects of our innate Divinity or essence. Whether you wish to connect with the energy of Archangel Michael for immediate and powerful support and strength or to clear and purify low vibrational energy that is limiting you, or whether you wish to connect to your own Inner Being, the synergy of the clear quartz combination will unfailingly support your heartfelt intention to be present in the moment and to be open to allow that which is there for you to flow to you.

- Please sit in your comfortable meditation position.

- If you have a question or a situation with which you would like clarity or guiding support, bring that to mind.

- If you have a favorite invocation or preferred ritual for connecting to your teachers, guides or Spirit, please use that which feels right for you.

- Place four drops of your combined Centaury and Green Spider Orchid flower essences and clear quartz crystal essence under the tongue, anoint your clear quartz with a drop of neroli and/or frankincense essential oils, inhale a few drops of the expansive neroli oil and/or the protecting spicy frankincense oil from a tissue or handkerchief and throughout the meditation if you feel inspired to do so, and hold your stone in lightly cupped hands.

- Settle into the position, close your eyes, and take a long, slow, deep breath, releasing any tension on the exhale. Repeat with two more breaths.

- Feeling relaxed, still, and present to the moment, please state your intentions. *I am present for all that is here for me. I am listening, and you are welcome.*

- Breathe and release any tension with a long exhalation.

- The soft sound of the breath mirrors the tranquil space of silence where inner peace and harmony are found. Feel the breath, hear the breath, and allow for any awareness of connection that follows.

- Feel deep appreciation and gratitude for this time of connection to a Divine messenger, teacher, or aspect of Oneness, and come out of the meditation whenever you are ready.

Please know that no matter what you feel or do not feel during the meditation, any question you have asked has been answered, any clarity you are seeking has been forthcoming, and any connection you desired has been facilitated by the synergy of the high vibrational combination of clear quartz crystal, frankincense or neroli essential oil, and the clear quartz, Centaury, and Green Spider Orchid essence blend, and Archangel Michael. Your conscious awareness of an ability to be assertive in whatever way feels right for you, to make fearless choices, and to embrace all that you are and then choose to be all that you are have been awakened and heightened. If this is not a familiar practice for you, please be reassured that enhanced connection is always facilitated and clarity and answers always provided. Sometimes guidance will flow into your consciousness during the practice, sometimes you will be inspired to pick up a particular book, or turn onto a certain radio or television channel, or bump into someone as you go about your day. The answers and clarity always flow, but we do not always get to micromanage how they come to us. Indeed, trusting in our inherent guidance will always deliver that which we seek in the quickest, most direct, and life-enhancing way ... we just need to trust.

Remember, it is in the smallest of moments that miracles happen and the clearing, fearlessness and empowerment of Michael and associated teachers and guides, including your Higher Self, facilitated through the synergy of the clear quartz combination is indeed inspired.

Quartz, Rose

TRADITIONAL CHAKRA ASSOCIATION
Heart (4th)

MAIN APPLICATIONS
Unconditional Love • Inner Peace
Adaptability • Self-worth

SYNERGISTIC COMBINATION
Crystal: Rose Quartz
Essential Oil: Frankincense
Flower Essences: Holly and Bush Fuchsia
Archangel: Haniel

Rose quartz is the stone of unconditional love: for receiving, giving, opening to, and teaching unconditional love—the true essence of what it is to love. It is the prime crystal for the heart chakra and transpersonal heart, and the stone of Divine or Universal Love: unconditional, nurturing, loving, gentle, consistent, and endless. It brings a sense of self-worth and self-respect—we feel worthy of unconditional love. The transpersonal heart chakra is located on the right-hand side of the chest and a little higher than our physical heart—it is always open, ever-receiving, and is what connects us to the loving energy of infinite consciousness, the Oneness of humanity, the Universal field, or that which the Buddhists call Mind. It is that which connects us all, and that which connects us to All That Is.

This beautiful soft pink stone facilitates deep inner peace and calm as we open to the infinite field of peace, tranquility, love, mercy, and compassion of All That Is.

All levels of the heart are purified and opened to facilitate deep inner healing that allows self-love—that which is so difficult for so many, and resisted by so many. Rose quartz encourages and enhances deep feelings of self-forgiveness, self-acceptance, self-worth, self-responsibility, and self-respect. It is always an inside job: we cannot have love, kindness, and compassion for another if we do not have it for ourselves; we cannot give what we do not have; we cannot do what we do not know. Living with loving kindness and compassion is self-empowering.

Rose quartz helps us attract love and relationships that serve us well; it also helps to restore harmony in existing relationships—harmony and trust that come from our own enhanced feelings of self-worth and self-belief.

It strengthens our ability to empathize with others and to be sensitive to the needs of ourselves, and the needs of others. Self-responsibility and self-acceptance, empathy and sensitivity, strengthen and empower us to adapt and accept change. Change is inevitable: those who cannot adapt cannot accept it; those who cannot adapt must endure it.

Rose quartz supports a decision to willingly release emotional pain, internalized pain from unexpressed emotions, and feelings of loss and deprivation. Energy is released, dissolved, and transmuted into pure positive energy for redistribution for the highest good.

The heart is open to receive love and to give love, to self and others, and to transmute negative feelings of being unlovable—we are loved, we are forgiven, we are able to love, we are able to forgive, and we are able to accept.

Gently holding rose quartz supports and strengthens daily affirmations by constantly drawing and replacing negative energy with positive life-affirming energy and supporting mindfulness of our intention as we go about the day.

Rose quartz can be worn or placed on the heart, thymus, or upper chest area—decorator stones can support a loving atmosphere when placed in a corner of any room.

How Rose Quartz Facilitates Well-Being

- Rose quartz is regarded as the finest emotional healer as unexpressed emotions and emotional pain are released and transmuted.

- It is calming and reassuring, helpful at times of crisis or any trauma, and supportive at times of change.

- It can bring great comfort in times of grief over lost love and heartache.

- Rose quartz helps to soothe pain and feelings of deprivation that have been internalized and held tight over time.

- Rose quartz encourages self-forgiveness and acceptance, and enhances self-worth, self-respect, self-responsibility, and self-trust.

. . . .

It is difficult to identify one "moment" with the rose quartz synergistic combination that would make sense in isolation; the synergistic combination, and before its creation some of its components, have been constant in my life for a number of years, possibly for longer than I am aware. When the components of most synergistic combinations came together so strongly, with such clear resonance, I could not help but smile, *of course*—they all made sense to me on a gut level, but rose quartz synergistic combination took me back to the early days of my current path.

The transformational gifts of this rose quartz synergistic combination and practices are the self-empowering choices of self-responsibility, self-acceptance, self-respect, and a sense of value or self-worth. It is all an inside job; it is all down to us, here, now, in this moment, to choose. I can still remember the compassion I felt for me when I truly accepted this and quieted my inner critic that had so often demanded the impossible—the ego can be such a voracious beast, and she is never satisfied.

I learned to accept that so much struggle and underlying sadness came from my attachment to how things should and should not be; I accepted responsibility for the deep pain I felt when relationships and situations were not as I wished or thought they should have been. They were what they were, and that core belief that they could be different if I was "better" had impacted me physically, mentally, and emotionally for a lifetime—hanging on to what another said or did, or should have said or done, twenty years ago drained so much energy! We spend so much of our lives trying to control the uncontrollable. Letting go was not always easy—but it was the greatest gift I could give myself.

Disliking ourselves is more harmful to the body than any food or drink. It is the most toxic thing we can do. It is self-destructive from the inside. The rose quartz synergistic combination can facilitate self-responsibility for change as we integrate loving kindness and compassion. Taking responsibility for me and accepting me, warts and all, has been life-enhancing in ways I could never have dreamed. There is great peace and joy in knowing we are so loved . . . and we are responsible.

Essential Oils, Flower Essences, and Spirit Connection

Rose quartz has long been a much-loved stone that is powerful on its own, but its potential benefits are magnified exponentially in combination. When we choose to explore the synergy of specific combinations, then we treat ourselves to the wonder that flows from a life grounded in adaptability and self-responsibility, and empowered by the heart.

Essential Oils

Rose essential oil has been cited by some practitioners as resonating with rose quartz. However, despite an undoubted resonance, the highest resonance is between frankincense essential oil and rose quartz. Frankincense and neroli resonate with quartz stones, but frankincense was clearly higher with this form of quartz. Traditionally, rose quartz is used with the heart chakra, but this power combination works effectively and synergistically to harmonize the whole being whether the crystal is placed on the body, held, worn, carried in the pocket, or placed nearby.

Frankincense (*Boswellia carterii* and *B. sacra*) is produced from the gum of the Boswellia tree in hot dry areas of the Mediterranean and Middle East. When the bark of the tree is damaged, the protective resinous gum, rich in essential oil, weeps from the trunk.

This spicy intoxicating oil has been prized across time for physical treatments and for religious and ritual ceremonies since the ancient world—the ancient Egyptians were using frankincense five thousand years ago. Biblical stories speak of Jesus being brought frankincense and myrrh at his birth, and Jesus anointed others with frankincense and myrrh throughout his life. Indeed, frankincense was as highly valued as precious gems and metals in ancient times, and was prized as an important part of ceremonial incenses. The name comes from two old French words which literally translate as "luxuriant incense." The true wonder of the aroma is revealed when the oil is warmed.

Apart from its wonderful cleansing, pain-relieving, healing, and protective properties for physical treatments, frankincense will stimulate and uplift, refresh and rejuvenate, or calm and sedate as required. It heals on all levels.

Psychologically it calms agitation, restlessness, anger, irritability, and panic; stimulates and uplifts lethargy, apathy, boredom, and despair; and rejuvenates one out of discouragement, disappointment, frustration, forgetfulness, and confusion.

On the emotional barometer, frankincense aligns with our spiritual body to shift our spirit from feeling vulnerable to feeling protected. The properties of this wonderfully woody, sweet, spicy fragrance attune to the subtle bodies and open us to Higher Self. Used to support meditation, frankincense will help to slow the breath and facilitate a quiet calm journey as one explores that which is within. This wonderful oil brings balance, stability, and protection to the heart that is vulnerable; our innate peaceful warrior is awakened, and we become aware and trusting of our inherent strength and inner protector and champion.

Flower Essences

The highest resonance is between rose quartz and Holly Bach Flower and Bush Fuchsia Australian Bush Flower Essences.

Universal Love is the essence of everything in this world; it is All That Is. The opposite of love is fear; fear, in all of its manifestations of negative emotion, such as hate, anger, jealousy, and revenge, is an absence of love. Just as darkness is simply an absence of light—we turn on the light; we cannot turn on the dark—so too fear is an absence of love. The two cannot exist in the same space at the same time.

Dr. Bach said, "Holly protects us from everything that is not Universal Love. Holly opens the heart and unites us with Divine Love," and Holly is often pivotal to healing. None of us is without any of these powerful negative feelings, either consciously in the moment, or unconsciously stored from the past and unexpressed, and so often these entrenched feelings become the basis of serious illness.

Holly is the remedy that embodies Universal Love, that all-encompassing love that is greater than all of us, that which sustains and nurtures every cell in every living being, and that which we all seek with every fiber of our being, that life force which constantly flows to us and through us. It is the antidote to hate which, at its core, is self-hate—and which, in turn, is either internalized or externalized.

The potential Holly transformation is one who lives in a state of grace with inner peace and harmony. There is a deep emotional understanding and tolerance of others; we radiate love and see others through the eyes of loving kindness and compassion.

Once we decide to allow the flow of Universal Love to carry us, to live in the river of life and go with the flow, we live in a state of grace—and grace is one of our innate gifts; it is always part of our own unique package.

Bush Fuchsia is the Australian Bush Flower Essence that allows us to follow our inner guidance and then speak our truth with courage and clarity. Once again, this flower essence connects us to the flow of Universal Love and is highly effective in helping to remove blockages that prevent the easy flow of voice, whether speaking with self or with others. An effective treatment for dyslexia, stuttering, and allaying nerves when speaking in public, this remedy also brings clarity of voice—clarity to our own inner voice, and clarity of voice as we share our truth with others and say how we feel.

The two hemispheres of the brain are balanced by Bush Fuchsia, restoring perfect balance between the logical left brain and the intuitive right brain functions. Balance between the two sides enhances our feelings of confidence and trust to heed the intuitive feelings that now flow with ease and clarity.

However the blockage to the free flow of speech presents, Bush Fuchsia brings courage to speak with clarity strengthened by self-acceptance and trust of our Inner Being and guidance; we speak our truth and express our true feelings with grace that flows with ease, freely and effortlessly.

Archangels

The highest resonance is between rose quartz and Archangel Haniel. Because it is similar to clear quartz, rose quartz also has a high resonance with Archangel Michael. However, clear quartz resonates highest with Archangel Michael, and rose quartz resonates highest with Archangel Haniel.

Archangel Haniel brings mystical, gentle, and beautifully supportive moon energy, energy of the Divine Feminine, gifting us grace that enhances our ability to hold a space, and find grace and poise to remain centered in any circumstance. This is no small feat!

Haniel's energy is very loving and healing. Indeed, Haniel is one of the four archangels who particularly facilitate healing, together with Michael, Raphael, and Uriel. All healing is facilitated: healing of self to embrace our own innate wellness and well-being; and healing abilities to help and facilitate wellness in others. Haniel particularly supports those who embrace natural healing, crystals, and harmonizing combinations from the Earth with the moon's energy.

Psychic abilities and intuition are enhanced; we are able to gracefully appreciate self and others, access the abundance of our inner wisdom and resources, feel the security of clear communication and guidance, see the inherent beauty and grace in All That Is, and feel the serenity of acceptance of what is.

The energy of Haniel is gentle and loving, but with power and support that is palpable as a cascading vibrational hum through the body. We feel empowered to accept self-responsibility, to embrace forgiveness and compassion, and to feel protected and supported as we adapt to the inevitable change that is inherent in the cycles of life. We choose to sing our own song and dance our own unique dance to the music of life in harmony with the vibrational hum of the Universe.

Meditation Practices

By choosing to quiet the mind with the rose quartz synergistic combination we feel deep inner peace and open to the power of self-responsibility and unconditional love as the physical integrates with the spiritual, through the mental and emotional bodies. We embrace a sense of wonder at the innate order, balance, and perfection in it all as we adapt to change and acknowledge self-worth. The infinite field of possibilities and potentialities is there for each of us. There is an elusive loving richness to a life that is regularly refreshed and aligned by quiet time alone in contemplation.

For the following meditations, please have at hand your crystal, essential oil, and crystal and flower essences. The crystal essence and combined flower essences may be taken in a single blend, or used separately, as is most convenient to you. The essential oil may certainly be vaporized in an oil burner to fill the meditation space, but as this is not always doable or convenient in some locations, please be assured that a few drops of essential oil on a tissue or handkerchief will serve you well at any time and in any location—whether meditating at home or in the park, or simply connecting in when nothing goes to plan.

Sit in whatever way is comfortable for you—if seated in a chair, have your feet flat on the floor with no shoes. Ensure your back is straight by gently lifting your heart center. Relax your shoulders. Lengthen the back of the neck by slightly tilting the chin downward.

Take a couple of breaths and bring yourself to a place of quiet appreciation of this time that you are gifting you.

Meditation to Connect with the Rose Quartz Synergy

Rose quartz is a much loved stone, and this is the easiest and "earthiest" of the three meditations using it in combination. In this meditation, we connect to the high vibrational energy that is created by the specific combination of these gifts from Mother Earth: rose quartz stone, frankincense essential oil, and a blend of rose quartz, Holly, and Bush Fuchsia essences. As always, it is all about the synergy of the combination. I use this meditation whenever I feel in need of the support, compassion, peace, and understanding that inevitably follow as I am calmed and uplifted. To connect with the rose quartz synergy, you will need:

Rose quartz crystal

Frankincense essential oil

Holly and Bush Fuchsia flower essences

Rose quartz crystal essence

- Place four drops of the combined Holly and Bush Fuchsia flower essences and rose quartz crystal essence under your tongue. Take a breath.

- Anoint the rose quartz with a drop of frankincense essential oil. Inhale the uplifting and intoxicating fragrance as you gently rub the oil into the stone, breathing slowly and deeply. Take a breath.

- Cup the rose quartz lightly in your hands—the fingertips of the right hand gently touch to the base of the left palm—and rest your hands comfortably in your lap. Take a breath and softly close your eyes.

- Feel the energy of the rose quartz as it fills your cupped hands—for example, it may feel tingling, effervescent, light, heavy, or like your hands are suctioned together or they may expand apart during the session—there is no right way it should feel, and how it feels is right for you.

- Feel or imagine the energy moving up through your arms, through to the heart center, and radiating out to fill your being in whatever way feels right for you.

- Trust that the synergy of the combination will lovingly calm, heal, open, or enhance that which needs attention at this time.

- You may see the pink of the rose quartz behind the closed eyes—maybe glittering flashes, maybe an expansive mist or swirls of color, or deep color that fades in and out, as the energy of the rose quartz combination connects with various energy centers.

- Feel gratitude for any loving strength, support, peace, or awareness that comes to you and let it go, trusting that it will be there for you when you come out of the meditation.

- Feel the energy. Be in wonder of the synergy of these combined gifts from Mother Earth. Luxuriate in the connection; allow it to lovingly fill you and empower you and remain within that expansive grounded space of love for as long as you wish.

Meditation on the Essence of the Rose Quartz Combination (with Affirmations)

The love and peace generated by this meditation makes this the most powerful of the three rose quartz meditations for supporting change. Love does make us strong, and a heartfelt decision to lovingly and willingly let go is a powerful catalyst for change. Again, it is all about the synergy of the combination that lifts the vibration of our physical, emotional, mental, and spiritual bodies, and the specific affirmations are an integral component of the synergy of this meditation practice. The affirmations allow and facilitate change in ways that continually surprise and delight me—the words remain unchanged each time, but the results are as different as I am each time I change and grow, and then return to this inspired rose quartz affirmation practice.

- Please sit in your comfortable meditation position.

- Place four drops of your combined Holly and Bush Fuchsia flower essences and rose quartz crystal essence under the tongue, anoint your rose quartz with a drop of frankincense essential oil and inhale a few drops of frankincense from a tissue or handkerchief while holding your stone in lightly cupped hands.

- Settle into the position, close your eyes, and take a long, slow, deep breath, releasing any tension on the exhale. Repeat with two more breaths.

- Take your awareness behind the eyebrow center. This is the third eye chakra. The color is deep indigo or purple. See yourself sitting in the middle of this space—the one in the middle who intuitively knows.

- Breathe.

- Take your awareness to the crown above you. See it layered with the petals of a closed lotus flower and imagine those petals unfolding, opening to pure positive energy and the infinite field of possibilities.

- Allow the pure white light to illuminate and enliven the deep indigo purple of this space. Feel the energy flood in and cascade through the physical body.

- Breathe.

- Repeat this statement to yourself. *I am loving and peaceful.*

- Breathe.

- Take your awareness to just below the navel center. This is the sacral chakra. The color is a rich orange. See the pelvic area as a golden bowl filled with the vibrant orange waters of creativity. You sit in the middle on a giant lotus leaf, perfectly balanced, fully supported.

- Breathe.

- No matter which way you choose to move, the liquid always returns to balance with you perfectly supported in the middle.

- Breathe.

- Repeat this statement to yourself. *I am fully supported as I adapt to change.*

- Breathe.

- Take your awareness to the chest center. This is the heart chakra—the middle chakra, that which bridges the upper three and lower three. The color is vibrant emerald or forest green. See yourself in the middle on a vibrant pink and white lotus flower atop a green lotus leaf. You are seated in your heart, the center of unconditional love.

- Breathe.

- See the heart center flooded with Divine energy from above as life-force energy rises to meet it from below. You are supported in Love from above and below.

- Repeat this statement to yourself. *I am gifted unconditional love and have infinite worth.*

- Breathe.

- This powerful energy from your heart center floods down your arms and out through your hands to touch the world. You are fully supported and in your power as you choose to act from your heart.

- Repeat the full affirmation, feeling Spirit, or your innate Divinity, Higher Self, or beautiful Inner Being speaking to you. *You are loving and peaceful, and fully supported as you adapt to change. You are gifted unconditional love and have infinite worth. You are energy being human.*

- Breathe. Remain in this space, feeling this space, for as long as it feels comfortable, or as long as your schedule allows.

- When you are ready, take a deep breath and bring your awareness back to the crown. See the petals of the lotus flower closing once again—yours to open at will, and close at will.

- Take another long, slow breath.

- Bring your awareness back into the body. Wiggle your toes and fingers, gently move your hands and your head, and open your eyes to bring your awareness fully back into this moment.

- Express gratitude for All That Is and the gift of grace ... and be aware that your Source is even more grateful for all that you are, and all that you are becoming. And so It is.

Meditation to Connect with Archangel Haniel, Higher Self, and Spirit Guides and Teachers

This simple meditation is often favored by those who already enjoy working with archangels, Spirit, guides, or teachers, but please remember that they are all aspects of our innate Divinity or essence. Whether you wish to connect with the energy of Archangel Haniel for unconditional support, grace, understanding, and compassion, or whether you wish to connect to your own Inner Being, the synergy of the rose quartz combination will powerfully support your heartfelt intention to be present in the moment and to be open to allow that which is there for you to flow to you.

- Please sit in your comfortable meditation position.

- Place four drops of your combined Holly and Bush Fuchsia flower essences and rose quartz crystal essence under the tongue, anoint your rose quartz with a drop of frankincense essential oil, inhale a few drops of the uplifting protection of the spicy frankincense oil from a tissue or handkerchief and throughout the meditation if you feel inspired to do so, and hold your stone in lightly cupped hands.

- Settle into the position, close your eyes, and take a long, slow, deep breath, releasing any tension on the exhale. Repeat with two more breaths.

- Feeling relaxed, still, and present to the moment, please state your intentions. *I am present for all that is here for me. I am listening, and you are welcome.*

- Breathe and release any tension with a long exhalation.

- The soft sound of the breath mirrors the tranquil space of silence where inner peace and harmony are found. Feel the breath, hear the breath, and allow for any awareness of connection that follows.

- Feel deep appreciation and gratitude for this time of connection to a Divine messenger, teacher, or aspect of Oneness, and come out of the meditation whenever you are ready.

Please know that no matter what you feel or do not feel during the meditation, any question you have asked has been answered, any clarity you are seeking has been forthcoming, and any connection you desired has been facilitated by the synergy of the high vibrational combination of rose quartz crystal, frankincense essential oil, and the rose quartz, Holly, and Bush Fuchsia essence blend, and Archangel Haniel. Your conscious awareness of the unconditional love that is there for you, of inner peace, of the strength of adaptability, and of your inherent self-worth have been awakened and heightened. If this is not a familiar practice for you, please be reassured that enhanced connection is always facilitated and clarity and answers always provided. Sometimes guidance will flow into your consciousness during the practice, sometimes you will be inspired to pick up a particular book, or turn onto a certain radio or television channel, or bump into someone as you go about your day. The answers and clarity always flow, but we do not always get to micromanage how they come to us. Indeed, trusting in our inherent guidance will always deliver that which we seek in the quickest, most direct, and life-enhancing way ... we just need to trust.

Remember, it is in the smallest of moments that miracles happen and the unconditional love, grace and poise of Haniel and associated teachers and guides, including your Higher Self, facilitated through the synergy of the rose quartz combination is indeed inspired.

Selenite

TRADITIONAL CHAKRA ASSOCIATION
Third Eye (6th) • Crown (7th) • Higher Crown (8th)

MAIN APPLICATIONS
Miracles • Inspired Choice • Innate Divinity
Shining Divinity through Humanity

SYNERGISTIC COMBINATION
Crystal: Selenite
Essential Oil: Neroli
Flower Essences: Elm and Bush Iris
Archangel: Gabriel

Selenite is named after Selene, the Greek goddess of the Moon, reflecting the moon-like glow of pure white selenite, which is gentle, cleansing, nurturing, and light-giving. Broadly, this magnificent stone is cleansing while bringing gentleness and light, enhancing communication and accessing the Angelic realm.

Beautiful selenite also comes in orange, blue, brown, and green—however, it is the pure white selenite that I use and is the focus of this information. This ancient stone is one of the most powerful crystals that I enjoy using.

This translucent stone has a very fine resonance that allows pure nurturing light to be channeled through to the crown chakra, therefore allowing access to the Archangelic realm and higher guidance with clear communication. The purest and most translucent white stones have such an ethereal or ghostly quality that they are said to inhabit that unearthly place between light and matter.

It connects to the subtle energy of the light body that supports our spirit and higher consciousness and anchors it to the vibration of Mother Earth—stagnant energy blockages are released, and deep peace surrounds us and flows through us.

It stimulates the brain, expands awareness, and brings clarity of mind; selenite symbolizes the highest clarity of mind we can attain.

We feel protected, centered, and in communication with our Higher Self and higher guidance and therefore feel the deep peace, calmness, and assuredness that comes from such connection. Selenite opens the crown and higher crown chakras. This stone emanates such calm that deep peace is always instilled.

It is therefore easy to see that selenite is an excellent aid for meditation or any spiritual work. Indeed, if two people each hold a stone, they both will experience enhanced telepathy. Selenite holds the imprint of all that ever has been, and all that is and ever will be, across space and time and reaches other lives; it can also be helpful for accessing the current life plan.

The protection offered by selenite can also be useful as a protective grid around the home—place a piece of selenite in each corner of the home to create a quiet space of high-frequency vibration shielded from outside negative influences. Alternatively, a large stone placed somewhere inside will ensure a tranquil atmosphere.

Selenite can be regarded as a transformational stone as old wounds are healed and negative energies are released and transmuted into pure positive energy leading to forgiveness and acceptance of what is, and an enhanced awareness to walk a new path.

How Selenite Facilitates Well-Being

- Selenite brings clarity of thought and mind, clearing confusion.

- It assists with judgment and enhances insight—we are able to see the bigger picture and come to a deeper conscious understanding.

- A selenite wand can detach unwanted vibrational beings from the aura.

- Emotionally, selenite will powerfully dispel and settle erratic emotions.

- Selenite grounds Divine Angelic energy, offering powerful healing to the Earth.

- This stone can help us identify lessons and issues that we are working on, subconsciously, and can show us the most direct, effective, and compassionate way forward.

....

The application of this synergistic combination may seem a little more ethereal, and the connections a little more eclectic, than many combinations—but to doubt the strength and grace gifted by the selenite synergistic combination would be a mistake. This synergistic combination is one that is particularly close to my heart and one that has supported much of the exponential growth that I have enjoyed at times.

Stuff happens... and I may just want to go to ground and wrap myself in a soft blanket, but with the support of the selenite synergistic combination, I will take another look, review the choices I have made, view it from broader perspective, and learn. Each of us is gifted free will; choices and decisions always bring consequences, which is how we learn and grow. We are encouraged to tread gently whether walking on Mother Earth or across another's path, leaving no footprints and little trace except the wisp of connection and support, appreciating the inherent circles and cycles, no beginning, no end.

It is so important to walk our talk. When we remain in integrity, express our Divinity through our heart, and celebrate all that we have become, and are ever becoming, we offer a beacon for others to say, *I want what she's got.* We all get to live our own miracle.

I do expect a miracle: life is a miracle, every exhalation a little death that is followed by a revitalizing inhalation. Our physical bodies are such magnificent mechanisms, constantly recalibrating to restore balance and so forgiving of our choices, that they truly are miraculous as they indicate and model for us. Indeed, there is a miracle in every moment.

I smile at the memory of another selenite miracle when I chose to support someone who I had learned did not genuinely wish me well and had not always been as they seemed. My decision to agree to her request came from standing in my integrity and holding clear intentions that only the highest good would be served, and trust that I would be protected by the selenite synergistic combination. I am sure you can imagine my warm smile when all went well, but the video they decided to make of the event failed to record. Yes, I expect a miracle.

Essential Oils, Flower Essences, and Spirit Connection

Selenite is ethereal, mystical, and, no doubt, powerful on its own, but the potentialities and possibilities that it can open for us are transformed when it is used in combination. When we choose to immerse ourselves in the synergy of the following combinations, we gift ourselves an appreciation of the wonder and miracle of life.

Essential Oils

Neroli, rosewood, and angelica essential oils have all been cited by other practitioners as resonating with selenite, particularly as it aligns with the higher crown, or eighth, chakra. However, the highest resonance is between neroli essential oil and selenite. Traditionally, selenite is used with the third eye, crown, and higher crown chakras, but this power combination works effectively and synergistically to harmonize the whole being whether the crystal is placed on the body, held, worn, carried in the pocket, or placed nearby.

The eighth, or higher crown, chakra is the center of the Higher Self, the one who "sits in the middle and knows" as poet Robert Frost beautifully described—it is that stillness within from where we reach out to the Divine. The energy is pure and expansive, therefore it should be no surprise that the oil that fully harmonizes with its purity and radiance is that extracted from the pure white blossoms of the bitter orange (*Citrus aurantium*): neroli. There is great affinity and harmony between neroli and the beautiful pure white stone, selenite, which radiates purity and refinement.

This precious essential oil is extracted by steam distillation of the fragrant flowers, as well as by the time-consuming enfleurage method using animal fat. Like jasmine and rose oils, neroli is not inexpensive to produce, with one hundred kilograms of flowers yielding one liter of the precious essential oil.

The delicate pale yellow neroli oil is profoundly calming to the physical body and will purify any environment: use it in a purifying bath or in a burner to purify your meditation space and allow for healing, or simply place a few drops on a tissue to inhale for immediate tranquility and reassuring reconnection.

This refreshing, relaxing, calming, and uplifting oil will calm a charged emotional state, uplift from anxiety and depression, and help with confusion, poor concentration, apathy, despair, despondency, lethargy, fear, irritability, jealousy, panic, shock, and restlessness... to mention but a few of its applications.

On the emotional barometer, neroli aligns with the spiritual body transforming the negative feelings of no choice into an expansive awareness of the unlimited choices that are available to us. This delightful fragrance bridges the subtle bodies, bringing renewal and alignment that encourages awareness of consequences, and considered and empowered choices. We are empowered to change, and that is no small feat!

Flower Essences

The highest resonance is between selenite and Elm Bach Flower and Bush Iris Australian Bush Flower Essences.

Elm is one of the Bach Flower Essences for despondency or despair. However, it is for those who are highly capable and intuitive but momentarily feel overwhelmed with the responsibility and scope of that which they feel is their life work—they are hit by self-doubt and a dip in self-confidence, troubled by feelings of inadequacy and not being up to the task, which then flows through to feelings of exhaustion and despondency. The indicative factor with Elm types is that the temporary feelings of inadequacy or loss of self-confidence are just that: temporary; we usually see Elm energy in the positive.

Elm types know that they are capable of doing whatever they have chosen to do; they feel they have chosen their life work, what they were meant to do, their life purpose, and they are capable of doing it well. However, sometimes they will feel completely overwhelmed by what they have chosen to do, its size and scope, and the responsibility that comes with it; they strive so hard to do what they do perfectly that exhaustion temporarily overcomes them and causes a spiral downward in body, mind, and spirit.

Thankfully, the downward spiral ends quickly as the wavering of self-confidence is fleeting. They soon return to balance supported by their innate knowing that they are doing what they are meant to be doing, their awareness of their innate connection, and their belief that we are never given more than we can handle. They feel fully supported by their innate connection, strength, and wisdom to see the job through to a successful completion.

The potential Elm transformation is one whose self-assurance and self-confidence is supported by an unshakable inner conviction that help is always available; the notable abilities of the Elm type are often guided by altruism—the work they feel driven to do is for the benefit of others, and that which can potentially make a difference.

Bush Iris is the Australian Blush Flower Essence for those who have lost their innate connection to their intuitive perception and the spiritual realm; it is also perfect for anyone who wishes to explore their spirituality or seeks support for opening up to, and enhancing, spiritual awareness.

The negative Bush Iris type tends to place too much importance on (and amassing) material possessions; they may be overly focused on the "good life" and indulging to excess in all manner of pleasures that do not serve them well. Bush Iris is also known to be helpful for those who are approaching death and are very fearful.

The potentially positive outcome with Bush Iris flows from clearing energy blockages in the base chakras—the rebalancing restores trust, enhances our innate connection and supports an awakening of spirituality. We feel attuned and aligned and supported by an enhanced awareness; creativity, creative visualization, and meditation are improved. Bush Iris helps us know that the Divine lives within us.

Archangels

The highest resonance is between selenite and Archangel Gabriel.

Archangel Gabriel has been depicted throughout history as both a male and female angel but, of course, this realm is without form and Gabriel, therefore, is neither male nor female. However, Gabriel has long been regarded as powerful and strong and I feel the strength, courage, and clear direction she brings as being that of the Divine Feminine—an inspirational coach who motivates us to overcome fear and procrastination, to follow our life purpose.

Gabriel is particularly helpful with all forms of communication—she powerfully supports us as we speak our truth. Traditionally, seen as the messenger angel and supporting parents and newborns, Gabriel also powerfully supports newborn creative projects—motivating, strengthening creativity, and opening doors of opportunity to bring ideas forth into reality. As a messenger of love, she powerfully supports, harmonizes and shields all who follow their life purpose and live from their heart. We become aware of the Divine Feminine, the creative Source, inherent within each of us.

She will encourage a change in perspective to see perceived problems from a broader view and clearing negative energy; compassion and understanding are assured, and lessons learned are clear. We are encouraged by clear direction and perseverance to stick to our life purpose, with awareness of miraculous manifestations and guiding intuition. There is balancing of yin and yang energies, globally and individually, and we are supported by inner peace, tranquility, and harmony. We become deeply aware of our innate Divinity—the Divine lives within us, and is expressed through our humanity. We are the miracle and so miracles flow through us.

Meditation Practices

By choosing to quiet the mind with the selenite synergistic combination, we become aware of the lack of pressure and inherent ease when we see ourselves as ordinary, no better or worse than the next, and then the reassuring flow that comes from choosing to live an extraordinary life, and the love and strength that comes from choosing to express our innate Divinity through our humanity; we can expect a miracle as the physical integrates with the spiritual. We embrace a sense of wonder at the innate order, balance, and perfection in it all. The infinite field of possibilities and potentialities is there for each of us. There is an elusive richness to a life that is regularly refreshed and aligned by quiet time alone in contemplation.

For the following meditations, please have at hand your crystal, essential oil, and crystal and flower essences. The crystal essence and combined flower essences may be taken in a single blend, or used separately, as is most convenient to you. The essential oil may certainly be vaporized in an oil burner to fill the meditation space, but as this is not always doable or convenient in some locations, please be assured that a few drops of essential oil on a tissue or handkerchief will serve you well at any time and in any location—whether meditating at home or in the garden, or simply connecting in while sitting at the bus stop.

Sit in whatever way is comfortable for you—if seated in a chair, have your feet flat on the floor with no shoes. Ensure your back is straight by gently lifting your heart center. Relax your shoulders. Lengthen the back of the neck by slightly tilting the chin downward.

Take a couple of breaths and bring yourself to a place of quiet appreciation of this time that you are gifting you.

Meditation to Connect with the Selenite Synergy

This is undoubtedly the simplest and "earthiest" of the three meditations connecting us to the ethereal wonder of selenite in combination. We connect to the high vibrational energy that is created by the specific combination of these gifts from Mother Earth: selenite stone, neroli essential oil, and a blend of selenite, Elm, and Bush Iris essences. As always, it is all about the synergy of the combination. I use this meditation whenever I feel in need of the clarity, connection, and knowing that inevitably follow as I am calmed and uplifted. To connect with the selenite synergy, you will need:

Selenite crystal

Neroli essential oil

Elm and Bush Iris flower essences

Selenite crystal essence

- Place four drops of the combined Elm and Bush Iris flower essences and selenite crystal essence under your tongue.
  Take a breath.

- Anoint the selenite with a drop of neroli essential oil. Inhale the delicately uplifting and purifying fragrance as you gently rub the oil into the stone, breathing slowly and deeply. Take a breath.

- Cup the selenite lightly in your hands—the fingertips of the right hand gently touch to the base of the left palm— and rest your hands comfortably in your lap. Take a breath and softly close your eyes.

- Feel the energy of the selenite as it fills your cupped hands— for example, it may feel tingling, effervescent, light, heavy, or like your hands are suctioned together or they may expand apart during the session—there is no right way it should feel, and how it feels is right for you.

- Feel or imagine the energy moving up through your arms, through to the heart center, and radiating out to fill your entire being in whatever way feels right for you.

- Trust that the synergy and miracle of the combination will uplift, heal, open, or enhance that which needs attention at this time.

- You may see the ethereal soft glow of the selenite behind the closed eyes—maybe glittering flashes, maybe an expansive mist or swirls of color, or color that fades in and out, as the energy of the selenite combination connects with various energy centers.

- Feel gratitude for any guiding strength, harmony, peace, awareness, or miracles that shine through to you and let them go, trusting that all will be there for you when you come out of the meditation.

- Feel the energy. Be in wonder of the synergy of these combined gifts from Mother Earth. Luxuriate in the connection that is ever present and shines through you; allow it to wondrously fill you, expand you, and guide you and remain within that expansive grounded space for as long as you wish.

Meditation on the Essence of the Selenite Combination (with Affirmations)

The delicate strength and connection facilitated by selenite in combination radiates through this meditation, the most powerful of the three selenite meditations for supporting change. Choosing to release limiting views is a potent catalyst for embracing a life well lived. Again, it is all about the synergy of the combination that lifts the vibration of our physical, emotional, mental, and spiritual bodies, and the specific affirmations are an integral component of the synergy of this meditation practice. The affirmations allow and facilitate change in ways that continually surprise and delight me—the words remain unchanged each time, but the results are as different as I am each time I change and grow, and then return to this inspired selenite affirmation practice.

- Please sit in your comfortable meditation position.

- Place four drops of your combined Elm and Bush Iris flower essences and selenite crystal essence under the tongue, anoint your selenite with a drop of neroli essential oil and inhale a few drops of neroli from a tissue or handkerchief while holding your stone in lightly cupped hands.

- Settle into the position, close your eyes, and take a long, slow, deep breath, releasing any tension on the exhale. Repeat with two more breaths.

- Take your awareness behind the eyebrow center. This is the third eye chakra. The color is deep indigo or purple. See yourself sitting in the middle of this space—the one in the middle who intuitively knows.

- Breathe.

- Take your awareness to the crown above you. See it layered with the petals of a closed lotus flower and imagine those petals unfolding, opening to pure positive energy and the infinite field of possibilities.

- Allow the pure white light to illuminate and enliven the deep indigo purple of this space. Feel the energy flood in and cascade through the physical body.

- Breathe.

- Repeat this statement to yourself. *I expect a miracle.*

- Breathe.

- Take your awareness to just below the navel center. This is the sacral chakra. The color is a rich orange. See the pelvic area as a golden bowl filled with the vibrant orange waters of creativity. You sit in the middle on a giant lotus leaf, perfectly balanced, fully supported.

- Breathe.

- No matter which way you choose to move, the liquid always returns to balance with you perfectly supported in the middle.

- Breathe.

- Repeat this statement to yourself. *I am ordinary but I can choose to live an extraordinary life.*

- Breathe.

- Take your awareness to the chest center. This is the heart chakra—the middle chakra, that which bridges the upper three and lower three. The color is vibrant emerald or forest green. See yourself in the middle on a vibrant pink and white lotus flower atop a green lotus leaf. You are seated in your heart, the center of unconditional love.

- Breathe.

- See the heart center flooded with Divine energy from above as life-force energy rises to meet it from below. You are supported in Love from above and below.

- Repeat this statement to yourself. *I shine my Divinity through my humanity.*

- Breathe.

- This powerful energy from your heart center floods down your arms and out through your hands to touch the world. You are fully supported and in your power as you choose to act from your heart.

- Repeat the full affirmation, feeling Spirit, or your innate Divinity, Higher Self, or beautiful Inner Being speaking to you. *Expect a miracle; you are ordinary but you can choose to live an extraordinary life. Your Divinity shines through your humanity. You are energy being human.*

- Breathe. Remain in this space, feeling this space, for as long as it feels comfortable, or as long as your schedule allows.

- When you are ready, take a deep breath and bring your awareness back to the crown. See the petals of the lotus closing once again—yours to open at will, and close at will.

- Take another long, slow breath.

- Bring your awareness back into the body. Wiggle your toes and fingers, gently move your hands and your head, and open your eyes to bring your awareness fully back into this moment.

- Express gratitude for All That Is and the gift of grace... and be aware that your Source is even more grateful for all that you are, and all that you are becoming. And so It is.

Meditation to Connect with Archangel Gabriel, Higher Self, and Spirit Guides and Teachers

This simple meditation is often favored by those who already enjoy working with archangels, Spirit, guides, or teachers, but please remember that they are all aspects of our innate Divinity or essence. Whether you wish to connect with the energy of Archangel Gabriel for strength, motivation, guidance, or clear communication, or whether you wish to connect to your own Inner Being, the synergy of the selenite combination will powerfully support your heartfelt intention to be present in the moment and to be open to allow that which is there for you to flow to you.

- Please sit in your comfortable meditation position.

- Place four drops of your combined Elm and Bush Iris flower essences and selenite crystal essence under the tongue, anoint your selenite with a drop of neroli essential oil, inhale a few drops of the expansive and purifying neroli oil from a tissue or handkerchief and throughout the meditation if you feel inspired to do so, and hold your stone in lightly cupped hands.

- Settle into the position, close your eyes, and take a long, slow, deep breath, releasing any tension on the exhale. Repeat with two more breaths.

- Feeling relaxed, still, and present to the moment, please state your intentions. *I am present for all that is here for me. I am listening, and you are welcome.*

- Breathe and release any tension with a long exhalation.

- The soft sound of the breath mirrors the tranquil space of silence where inner peace and harmony are found. Feel the breath, hear the breath, and allow for any awareness of connection that follows.

- Feel deep appreciation and gratitude for this time of connection to a Divine messenger, teacher, or aspect of Oneness, and come out of the meditation whenever you are ready.

Please know that no matter what you feel or do not feel during the meditation, any question you have asked has been answered, any clarity you are seeking has been forthcoming, and any connection you desired has been facilitated by the synergy of the high vibrational combination of selenite crystal, neroli essential oil, and selenite, Elm, and Bush Iris essence blend, and Archangel Gabriel. Your conscious awareness of the miracles that spring from the miracle that is life, of making inspired choices, and of your innate Divinity and the wonder of choosing to shine your Divinity through your humanity have been awakened and heightened. If this is not a familiar practice for you, please be reassured that enhanced connection is always facilitated and clarity and answers always provided. Sometimes guidance will flow into your consciousness during the practice, sometimes you will be inspired to pick up a particular book, or turn onto a certain radio or television channel, or bump into someone as you go about your day. The answers and clarity always flow, but we do not always get to micromanage how they come to us. Indeed, trusting in our inherent guidance will always deliver that which we seek in the quickest, most direct, and life-enhancing way ... we just need to trust.

Remember, it is in the smallest of moments that miracles happen and the purity, strength, guidance and voice of Gabriel and associated teachers and guides, including your Higher Self, facilitated through the synergy of the selenite combination is indeed inspired.

Tiger Iron

TRADITIONAL CHAKRA ASSOCIATION
Base (1st) • Sacral (2nd) • Solar Plexus (3rd)
Linking lower Chakras to Crown (7th)

MAIN APPLICATIONS
Knowing self • Grace and Poise
Nurtured and Sustained • Peaceful Warrior

SYNERGISTIC COMBINATION
Crystal: Tiger Iron
Essential Oil: Frankincense
Flower Essences: Walnut and Red Grevillea
Archangel: Haniel

Tiger iron is a naturally occurring composite stone from the layering of sedi-
mentary deposits over billions of years—it is comprised of tiger's eye, red jasper, and hematite. Its name derives from tiger's eye and the iron-rich hematite,
and while it may not be the prettiest of stones, the intrinsic layer patterning
gives an earthy beauty.

Although uniquely its own stone with its own resonance, it also brings the
significant properties of its individual parts—but like any synergistic combination, the whole is so much more than the sum of its parts.

Tiger iron stimulates the base, sacral, and solar plexus chakras, revitalizing and strengthening our ability to survive, create, and thrive. It enhances strength, vitality, and energy, while motivating willpower, tenacity, and confidence to follow through. At the same time, it stimulates and supports the lower chakras, it also resonates with the crown chakra thereby facilitating an opening to Higher Self—we become aware of being fully supported to survive and thrive with the grace that is inherent in all our gifts.

It stimulates creativity, often revealing and developing previously hidden talents—it merges creativity with focus, motivating one to complete the creative project.

Tiger iron powerfully supports change, that which is integral to all, and yet that with which so many struggle. However, when we accept self-responsibility, this stone helps clear space to see what is required from a broader perspective. We feel encouraged to change or adapt; we feel empowered to take required action; we feel fully supported as we move through the process of change; a sense of refuge is constant if the going gets tough; the power to discern and discriminate as we change and grow is recognized; we feel protected and strong. Interestingly, while tiger iron stimulates artistic creativity, the higher guidance that supports change brings solutions that are pragmatic, down-to-earth, simple, and eminently doable—wonderful for those suffering mental and emotional stress.

Red jasper, "the supreme nurturer" powerfully balancing Mother Earth and the Divine, is discussed earlier. However, tiger's eye and hematite are not, and so a brief overview of the qualities that each brings to the whole might be helpful.

The dark brown tiger's eye, with its golden bands, resonates with the base and crown chakras, reflecting the connection between the Divine and Gaia—the God above, and Goddess below—and facilitating integration, order, stability, and prosperity, and enhancing our innate personal power and ability to act from a place of authenticity.

The dark silver-grey hematite resonates with the power, protection, and grounding of the base chakra, while facilitating access to Divine knowing. It harmonizes every level; we are grounded, centered, and strong. Negative energies are dissolved; those who build mountains from molehills, or become bogged down in how things should or should not be, feel great relief.

How Tiger Iron Facilitates Well-Being

- Tiger iron powerfully supports change, courage and discernment: enhancing ability to change; empowering required action; bringing awareness to take refuge if needed.

- It enhances willpower, focus, and mental clarity— and opens creativity.

- Intuition is enhanced—solutions are pragmatic and simple; we thrive with grace.

- Tiger iron is particularly helpful for stress or emotional and/ or mental burnout.

- We embrace the breathtaking power of the Divine Feminine and Masculine.

············

It was intriguing to me that I should be initially so drawn to this stone: it was previously unknown to me; the name of it resonated through my pendulum as I scoured a list of crystals from a new supplier. Tiger iron, visually so easily overlooked, opened many channels for me once I prepared it with the frankincense essential oil with which it so powerfully resonated. The synergy of this combination has been pivotal to so much of my recent growth that has facilitated vibrational wellness and well-being on every level. I feel strong, empowered, and expansive with the tiger iron synergistic combination and I am ever mindful and in wonder of the synchronicity that brought me to the stone.

The inner strength and direction that this synergistic combination brought into my awareness was interesting: I felt such a powerful resonance, loved the daily meditations, and was aware of ongoing shifts that seemed to be facilitated by my embracing the process. However, I resisted including tiger iron in the new practice that I was sharing and constantly sought an alternative crystal: one that would be easier for others to source in their local crystal shops; one that might be visually more engaging and therefore those who would benefit would be more likely to be drawn to it.

In retrospect, it was truly astounding how I kept "checking in" for an alternative—my head was saying "there must be something better," while my heart and body were resonating with the perfection of the synergistic combination. I seemed to be endeavoring to improve on perfection—and we all know what a self-defeating strategy that is!

Once I decided to lovingly and willingly release all of this struggle, to bring awareness to what was being highlighted, gratefully accept the guidance I was being gifted, and stop micromanaging what every other person might or might not see, say, feel, find, or do, I felt a peaceful strength that, for me, reflected the complementary dualities of the Divine Feminine and Masculine. I chose to act from a place of authenticity and was gifted new-found strength to walk my talk and hold the space, and to simply practice and share that which felt right for me as a powerful healing practice.

Essential Oils, Flower Essences, and Spirit Connection

Tiger iron is a powerful stone that offers great possibilities on its own. However, to combine the complexity of tiger iron with the following gifts is to unleash synergy that transforms and empowers as we bask in the support of the feminine and masculine perfectly poised in their Divine dance within.

Essential Oils

The highest resonance is between tiger iron and frankincense essential oil. Traditionally, tiger iron is used with the base, sacral, and solar plexus chakras, linking them to the crown chakra. However, this power combination works effectively and synergistically to harmonize the whole being whether the crystal is placed on the body, held, worn, carried in the pocket, or placed nearby.

Frankincense (*Boswellia carterii and B. sacra*) is produced from the gum of the Boswellia tree in hot dry areas of the Mediterranean and Middle East. When the bark of the tree is damaged, the protective resinous gum, rich in essential oil, weeps from the trunk.

This spicy intoxicating oil has been prized across time for physical treatments and for religious and ritual ceremonies since the ancient world—the Ancient Egyptians were using frankincense five thousand years ago. Biblical stories speak of Jesus being brought frankincense and myrrh at his birth and, throughout his life, Jesus anointed others with frankincense and myrrh. Indeed, frankincense was as highly valued as precious gems and metals in ancient times, and was prized as an important part of ceremonial incenses. The name comes from two old French words that literally translate as "luxuriant incense." The true wonder of the aroma is revealed when the oil is warmed.

Apart from its wonderful cleansing, pain-relieving, healing, and protective properties for physical treatments, frankincense will stimulate and uplift, refresh and rejuvenate, or calm and sedate as required. It heals on all levels.

Psychologically it calms agitation, restlessness, anger, irritability, and panic; stimulates and uplifts lethargy, apathy, boredom, and despair; and rejuvenates one out of discouragement, disappointment, frustration, forgetfulness, and confusion.

On the emotional barometer, frankincense aligns with the spiritual body to shift our spirit from feeling vulnerable to feeling protected. The properties of this wonderfully woody, sweet, spicy fragrance attune to the subtle bodies and open us to Higher Self; used to support meditation, frankincense will help to slow the breath and facilitate a quiet calm journey as one explores that which is within. This wonderful oil brings balance, stability, and protection to the heart that is vulnerable; our innate peaceful warrior is awakened, and we become aware and trusting of our inherent strength and inner protector and champion.

Flower Essences

The highest resonance is between tiger iron and Walnut Bach Flower and Red Grevillea Australian Bush Flower Essences.

Walnut is the protection Bach Flower Essence; it is the "link breaker" that frees us from the bondage of past or current events, traumas, ties with others, or habits that do not serve us well and serve only to hinder us from being all that we choose to be.

New beginnings are difficult, and moving on is often traumatic, when we find ourselves still ruled, restricted, caught up, or held back, often unconsciously, by old decisions, thoughts, habits, and entrenched negative patterns. The negative Walnut person is swayed by the ideas and influences of stronger, more dominant or persuasive personalities—goals or dreams remain unfulfilled and memories are filled with regret.

Walnut helps us move through times of change in our lives and supports us as we move forward—change of lifestyle, change of circumstances, change of direction, change of job, change of house, and all life transition stages, such as birth, starting school, puberty, marriage, divorce, and menopause. It supports times of change, helping us to move forward being true to ourselves, and move on from the past.

The potential transformation of Walnut brings a sense of protection and safety that allows us to follow our inner inspiration. The aura is strengthened and the binding shadow of the past is broken; we feel empowered to stay true to our Inner Being, to our true self, and move on with calm determination, no longer limited or influenced by the opinions of others.

Red Grevillea is for those who feel stuck, unable to move forward, and those who are overly sensitive to the critical opinions of others and are easily affected by others who are disagreeable and simply unpleasant to be around. The negative Red Grevillea person feels stuck: they know moving on or changing circumstances would enhance their lives; they know *what* to do, but they do not know *how* to do it.

Potential transformation of Red Grevillea is indeed powerful: one is strengthened to move on from situations that do not serve them well, and dependence on those who do not serve them well is released. Dependence is replaced by independence; timidity is replaced by boldness; sensitivity to the judgment and opinions of others is replaced by indifference that is supported by one's own inner resources.

Powerful Red Grevillea is indeed effective but it is also interesting to note that the path forward is not always that which would seem the most direct route. It does not serve us well to hold attachment, judgment, or firm expectation as to a particular way forward—sometimes we need to circle around, or even take a step or two back, in order to extricate ourselves from that which binds us and move forward in a way that best serves us on every level.

Archangels

The highest resonance is between tiger iron and Archangel Haniel.

Archangel Haniel brings mystical, gentle, and beautifully supportive moon energy, energy of the Divine Feminine, gifting us grace that enhances our ability to hold a space, and find grace and poise to remain centered in any circumstance. This is no small feat and great backup for a job interview, public presentation, event, or even a first date.

Haniel enhances healing, and indeed, is one of the four Archangels who particularly facilitate healing: Michael, Raphael, Uriel, and Haniel. All healing is facilitated: healing of self to embrace our own innate wellness and wellbeing; and healing abilities to help and facilitate wellness in others. Haniel particularly supports those who embrace natural healing, crystals, and harmonizing combinations from the Earth with the moon's energy.

Psychic abilities and intuition are enhanced. We are able to gracefully appreciate self and others, access the abundance of our inner wisdom and resources, feel the security of clear communication and guidance, see the inherent beauty and grace in All That Is, and feel the serenity of acceptance of what is.

The energy of Haniel is gentle and loving, but with power and support that is palpable as a tingling cascade through the body to the toes, down the back, or across the shoulders—we feel Spirit "has our back." Haniel brings awareness of the power, beauty, and strength of the Divine Feminine, helping with issues of self-empowerment, self-worth, and self-esteem. The energy brings great focus and wisdom, and enhances joy, love, natural healing, a sense of abundance, and appreciation of the natural cycles inherent in all, thereby helping us to transition and embrace that which serves our highest good.

•••••••••••••

It was many years ago that I first heard the Zen Buddhist story, *Is That So*— briefly, for those who might be unfamiliar, it tells of a monk who is falsely accused a number of times and answers each accusation with the simple question, *Is that so?* Many years pass, but in the end, the false accusations are proved false when accusers admit what they have done—and even when apologies and kindnesses are given to the monk he still replies, *Is that so?* I can still recall how this story touched me: I felt in absolute wonder of how it would be to not engage and to maintain that type of equanimity and acceptance of what is.

Tiger iron synergistic combination brings me the strength of Spirit and the grace of Haniel to stand in the shoes of the peaceful warrior and not engage, to stand in my own truth and allow others to stand where they choose, to have the courage to follow my passion and be me—it is the closest I have come to living the above story, which I have for so long held in wonder.

Once I chose this path and decided to embrace and integrate the synergistic practices, my spiritual growth has been fast-tracked, unexpected, joyful, and often confronting as I left the scenic route, at last. I am often tested to simply hold the space and not engage, and every so often it is ramped up a tad as I grow stronger—and I take this opportunity to express genuine gratitude for those who play their parts in facilitating these moments for me.

For one who has vacillated between living in the shadow of what others think, of getting it wrong, and standing to fight in full celebration of my fiery fire sign in poorly chosen battles that left me swamped by pain and guilt, I find it impossible to describe the peace, joy, and pure exhilaration of choosing the way of the peaceful warrior and holding my space with the palpable supreme strength of Spirit and the grace of Haniel that is facilitated by the tiger iron synergistic combination.

Meditation Practices

By choosing to quiet the mind with the tiger iron synergistic combination we open up to be realigned and attuned, as the physical integrates with the spiritual, through the mental and emotional bodies. We embrace a sense of wonder at the innate order, balance, and perfection in it all as we feel the perfect balance of the Divine Feminine and Masculine flowing through us. We are empowered by the heart of the peaceful warrior and appreciate that the infinite field of possibilities and potentialities is there for each of us. There is an elusive richness to a life that is regularly refreshed and aligned by quiet time alone in contemplation.

For the following meditations, please have at hand your crystal, essential oil, and crystal and flower essences. The crystal essence and combined flower essences may be taken in a single blend, or used separately, as is most convenient to you. The essential oil may certainly be vaporized in an oil burner to fill the meditation space, but as this is not always doable or convenient in some locations, please be assured that a few drops of essential oil on a tissue or handkerchief will serve you well at any time in any place—

whether meditating at home or in the park, or simply connecting in because the moment calls for it.

Sit in whatever way is comfortable for you—if seated in a chair, have your feet flat on the floor with no shoes. Ensure your back is straight by gently lifting your heart center. Relax your shoulders. Lengthen the back of the neck by slightly tilting the chin downward.

Take a couple of breaths and bring yourself to a place of quiet appreciation of this time that you are gifting you.

Meditation to Connect with the Tiger Iron Synergy

Many will find this the most straightforward and "earthy" of the three tiger iron meditations. In this meditation, we connect to the high vibrational energy that is created by the specific combination of these gifts from Mother Earth: tiger iron stone, frankincense essential oil, and a blend of tiger iron, Walnut, and Red Grevillea essences. As always, it is all about the synergy of the combination. I use this meditation whenever I feel in need of the stability, balance, and quiet inner strength that inevitably follow as I am calmed and uplifted. To connect with the tiger iron synergy, you will need—

Tiger iron crystal

Frankincense essential oil

Walnut and Red Grevillea flower essences

Tiger iron crystal essence

- Place four drops of the combined Walnut and Red Grevillea flower essences and tiger iron crystal essence under your tongue. Take a breath.

- Anoint the tiger iron with a drop of frankincense essential oil. Inhale the uplifting and deeply intoxicating fragrance as you gently rub the oil into the stone, breathing slowly and deeply. Take a breath.

- Cup the powerful tiger iron lightly in your hands, feeling its inherent density, complexity and strength—the fingertips of the right hand gently touch to the base of the left palm—and rest your hands comfortably in your lap. Take a breath and softly close your eyes.

- Feel the energy of the tiger iron as it fills your cupped hands—for example, it may feel tingling, effervescent, light, heavy, or like your hands are suctioned together or they may expand apart during the session—there is no right way it should feel, and how it feels is right for you.

- Feel or imagine the energy moving up through your arms, through to the heart center, and radiating out to fill your entire being in whatever way feels right for you.

- Trust that the synergy, power, and unity of the combination will unify, calm, heal, balance, open, or enhance that which needs attention at this time.

- You may see various colors behind the closed eyes—maybe glittering flashes, maybe deep swirls of spiraling color, or color that fades in and out, as the energy of the tiger iron combination connects with various energy centers.

- Feel gratitude for any guiding strength, harmony, awareness, or feelings of empowerment that come to you and let them go, trusting that all will be there, perfectly poised and within you when you come out of the meditation.

- Feel the energy. Be in wonder of the synergy of these combined gifts from Mother Earth. Luxuriate in the connection that is ever present and part of you; allow it to wondrously fill you, strengthen you, and expand you and remain within that expansive grounded space for as long as you wish.

Meditation on the Essence of the
Tiger Iron Combination (with Affirmations)

Without a doubt, of the three tiger iron meditations, this is the power meditation for supporting change and an ability to stand in our power and hold the space. We feel protected and empowered in the heart to let go of all that has kept us in restriction and limitation. Again, it is all about the synergy of the combination that lifts the vibration of our physical, emotional, mental, and spiritual bodies, and the specific affirmations are an integral component of the synergy of this meditation practice. The affirmations allow and facilitate change in ways that continually surprise and delight me—the words remain unchanged each time, but the results are as different as I am each time I change and grow, and then return to this inspired tiger iron affirmation practice.

- Please sit in your comfortable meditation position.

- Place four drops of your combined Walnut and Red Grevillea flower essences and tiger iron crystal essence under the tongue, anoint your tiger iron with a drop of frankincense essential oil and inhale a few drops of frankincense from a tissue or handkerchief while holding your stone in lightly cupped hands.

- Settle into the position, close your eyes, and take a long, slow, deep breath, releasing any tension on the exhale. Repeat with two more breaths.

- Take your awareness behind the eyebrow center. This is the third eye chakra. The color is deep indigo or purple. See yourself sitting in the middle of this space—the one in the middle who intuitively knows.

- Breathe.

- Take your awareness to the crown above you. See it layered with the petals of a closed lotus flower and imagine those petals unfolding, opening to pure positive energy and the infinite field of possibilities.

- Allow the pure white light to illuminate and enliven the deep indigo purple of this space. Feel the energy flood in and cascade through the physical body.

- Breathe.

- Repeat this statement to yourself. *Goddess/God lives within me, as me.*

- Breathe.

- Take your awareness to just below the navel center. This is the sacral chakra. The color is a rich orange. See the pelvic area as a golden bowl filled with the vibrant orange waters of creativity. You sit in the middle on a giant lotus leaf, perfectly balanced, fully supported.

- Breathe.

- No matter which way you choose to move, the liquid always returns to balance with you perfectly supported in the middle.

- Breathe.

- Repeat this statement to yourself. *I am perfectly poised in the dance of the Divine Feminine and Masculine.*

- Breathe.

- Take your awareness to the chest center. This is the heart chakra—the middle chakra, that which bridges the upper three and lower three. The color is vibrant emerald or forest green. See yourself in the middle on a vibrant pink and white lotus flower atop a green lotus leaf. You are seated in your heart, the center of unconditional love.

- Breathe.

- See the heart center flooded with Divine energy from above as life-force energy rises to meet it from below. You are supported in Love from above and below.

- Repeat this statement to yourself. *I am nurtured, sustained and protected by the heart of the peaceful warrior.*

- Breathe.

- This powerful energy from your heart center floods down your arms and out through your hands to touch the world. You are fully supported and in your power as you choose to act from your heart.

- Repeat the full affirmation, feeling Spirit, or your innate Divinity, Higher Self, or beautiful Inner Being speaking to you. *Goddess/God lives within you, as you. You are perfectly poised in the dance of the Divine Feminine and Masculine. You are nurtured, sustained, and protected by the heart of the peaceful warrior. You are energy being human.*

- Breathe. Remain in this space, feeling this space, for as long as it feels comfortable, or as long as your schedule allows.

- When you are ready, take a deep breath and bring your awareness back to the crown. See the petals of the lotus flower closing once again—yours to open at will, and close at will.

- Take another long, slow breath.

- Bring your awareness back into the body. Wiggle your toes and fingers, gently move your hands and your head, and open your eyes to bring your awareness fully back into this moment.

- Express gratitude for All That Is and the gift of grace ... and be aware that your Source is even more grateful for all that you are, and all that you are becoming. And so It is.

Meditation to Connect with Archangel Haniel, Higher Self, and Spirit Guides and Teachers

This simple meditation is often favored by those who already enjoy working with archangels, Spirit, guides, or teachers, but please remember that they are all aspects of our innate Divinity or essence. Whether you wish to connect with the energy of Archangel Haniel for grace, strength, and support, or whether you wish to connect to your own Inner Being, the synergy of the tiger iron combination will powerfully support your heartfelt intention to be present in the moment and to be open to allow that which is there for you to flow to you.

- Please sit in your comfortable meditation position.

- Place four drops of your combined Walnut and Red Grevillea flower essences and tiger iron crystal essence under the tongue, anoint your tiger iron with a drop of frankincense essential oil, inhale a few drops of the uplifting and protecting spicy frankincense oil from a tissue or handkerchief and throughout the meditation if you feel inspired to do so, and hold your stone in lightly cupped hands.

- Settle into the position, close your eyes, and take a long, slow, deep breath, releasing any tension on the exhale. Repeat with two more breaths.

- Feeling relaxed, still, and present to the moment, please state your intentions. *I am present for all that is here for me. I am listening, and you are welcome.*

- Breathe and release any tension with a long exhalation.

- The soft sound of the breath mirrors the tranquil space of silence where inner peace and harmony are found. Feel the breath, hear the breath, and allow for any awareness of connection that follows.

- Feel deep appreciation and gratitude for this time of connection to a Divine messenger, teacher, or aspect of Oneness, and come out of the meditation whenever you are ready.

Please know that no matter what you feel or do not feel during the meditation, any question you have asked has been answered, any clarity you are seeking has been forthcoming, and any connection you desired has been facilitated by the synergy of the high vibrational combination of tiger iron crystal, frankincense essential oil, and the tiger iron, Walnut, and Red Grevillea essence blend, and Archangel Haniel. Your conscious awareness and acceptance of knowing self, of the grace and poise that is within you, and of feeling nurtured and sustained by the powerful peaceful warrior that is the essence of you have been awakened and heightened. If this is not a familiar practice for you, please be reassured that enhanced connection is always facilitated and clarity and answers always provided. Sometimes guidance will flow into your consciousness during the practice, sometimes you will be inspired to pick up a particular book, or turn onto a certain radio or television channel, or bump into someone as you go about your day. The answers and clarity always flow, but we do not always get to micromanage how they come to us. Indeed, trusting in our inherent guidance will always deliver that which we seek in the quickest, most direct, and life-enhancing way ... we just need to trust.

Remember, it is in the smallest of moments that miracles happen and the empowering grace and harmony of Haniel and associated teachers and guides, including your Higher Self, facilitated through the synergy of the powerful tiger iron combination is indeed inspired.

Tourmaline, Black

TRADITIONAL CHAKRA ASSOCIATION
Base (1st) • Sacral (2nd) • Solar Plexus (3rd)

MAIN APPLICATIONS
Creativity • Infinite Possibilities
Infinite Potentialities • Living Our Divinity

SYNERGISTIC COMBINATION
Crystal: Black Tourmaline
Essential Oil: Lemon
Flower Essences: Willow and Kapok Bush
Archangel: Raziel

Tourmaline comes in various colors and all share the same life-enhancing qualities. However, some particular colors offer additional attributes that further expand the usefulness of this stone, and this particular synergistic combination will feature black tourmaline, also known as schorl. It is a powerful shamanic stone, traditionally used across the ages for scrying and healing.

Tourmaline balances and aligns our mental talents, energy centers, and biomagnetic field—a biomagnetic field surrounds every living thing. This stone protects, cleanses, purifies, transforms, and transmutes heavy dense energy into a lighter, higher frequency vibration. As mentioned, the tourmalines clear and rebalance all the energy centers, and black tourmaline resonates particularly powerfully with the lower three chakras: base, sacral, and solar plexus. Balance in these three chakras enhances our abilities to survive and thrive, create, and embrace self-responsibility, self-respect, and the power of self-will. Black tourmaline removes negative energy blockages from the subtle bodies.

A black tourmaline wand, pointed away from the body, will draw off negative energy to be transmuted into pure positive energy for the highest good. Remember, each of us is gifted free will, and our intention to lovingly and willingly release negative energy enhances the clearing vibrations of tourmaline—else we will soon replace that which has been drawn off with some other manifestation of that same negative energy.

This stone takes us deep inside ourselves, which some may find uncomfortable. But, this powerfully healing energy facilitates understanding and forgiveness of self and others. Self-worth, self-confidence, and self-responsibility are enhanced as fears are diminished, particularly when released with intent. Victimhood is banished, and then understanding, tolerance, compassion, kindness to self and others, and a sense of abundance and prosperity, are all embraced.

Black tourmaline is perhaps the ultimate protecting and grounding crystal—it absorbs and dissolves all forms of negative energy from psychic attack to negative thoughts to environmental radiation. This powerful stone focuses and strengthens body, mind, and spirit, and attracts the positive: rub black tourmaline to intensify its magnetic charge for luck, prosperity, and happiness. Tourmaline makes a powerful and effective crystal essence.

How Black Tourmaline Facilitates Well-Being

- Tourmaline enhances understanding, communication, and cooperation—with self and others—and brings a deeper appreciation of our true self.

- Self-confidence and a sense of self-respect are promoted as fear decreases when we no longer choose to see ourselves as victims.

- Renewed self-worth promotes a sense of loving kindness and compassion, tolerance, inspiration, and prosperity.

- Tourmaline balances the left and right sides of the brain and facilitates a different perspective as it transmutes negative thought patterns into the positive.

- Black tourmaline encourages a positive attitude in all situations, together with clarity of thought, and rational and logical thinking.

- Black tourmaline often awakens a sense of altruism, accompanied by practical creativity and action—our Divinity shines through our humanity.

- Black tourmaline encourages a more relaxed attitude to life that comes from true acceptance of what is and a sense of neutrality to outside events as we perceive the innate perfection in it all.

. . . .

Situations often come out of left field to energetically sideswipe us, just to remind us of old tendencies and vulnerabilities that still bubble beneath the surface—and they can give us truly delicious opportunities to shift out of entrenched negative beliefs. In all of these instances, I find the black tourmaline synergistic combination a powerfully supportive combination.

When we choose this path of self-responsibility and awareness, and if we choose to integrate that which we learn, we always grow. So, each time I reached for my unfairness shawl, hurt by something another did or did not do or say, it was but a blip in time, a fleeting revisit to the shadow of an old memory. I had moved on. Wow, what a shift that realization is!

The black tourmaline synergistic combination has supported me as the stone took me deep inside to forgive myself and others, and lovingly and willingly release lingering self-sabotaging issues of self-worth. I have been able to appreciate the inherent gifts of self-appraisal, discrimination, discernment, and strength that can come from insecurity and self-doubts that have been acknowledged, accepted, and released. I have come to own my shadow side, and avenues have since magically appeared and synchronistic doors swung open to opportunities to satisfy my curiosities in ways I could not have imagined!

This powerful black tourmaline synergistic combination supported the unraveling of many issues that had been triggered, with opportunities for forgiveness, and exponential growth that are still a wonder to me. Victimhood was banished, and subsequently understanding, tolerance, compassion, and kindness, and a sense of abundance and prosperity, were all fully embraced. I have been very blessed by the synergy of the black tourmaline combination; sometimes we do not fully appreciate the pain until it has gone.

Essential Oils, Flower Essences, and Spirit Connection

Black tourmaline powerfully enhances our being very well on its own, but there is unimagined versatility when used in combination. The synergy of the following combinations encourages a sense of magic and wonder that will encourage and delight you as you go forward embracing all that you are.

Essential Oils

Vetiver has been cited by others as resonating with black tourmaline, particularly as it aligns with the base, sacral, and solar plexus chakras. However, while there is good resonance with vetiver, the unquestionably highest resonance is between black tourmaline and lemon essential oil. Traditionally, black tourmaline is used with the base, sacral, and solar plexus chakras, but this power combination works effectively and synergistically to harmonize the whole being whether the crystal is placed on the body, held, worn, carried in the pocket, or placed nearby.

Lemon essential oil is cold-pressed from the peel of the fruit that follow the fragrant white flowers of the lemon (*Citrus limon*) tree. The tangy lemon is cultivated across the globe and, for the most part, the essential oil is still extracted by hand expression, with the green fruit yielding more than the sunny yellow skin of ripe fruit—around three thousand lemons produce one liter of essential oil.

Lemon essential oil cleanses, detoxifies, refreshes, stimulates, and rebalances our thoughts and emotions, as well as our physical body where it invigorates the immune system, and so much more. The scintillating aroma of lemon essential oil helps with anger, despair, discouragement, frustration, jealousy, lethargy, concentration, and unhelpful thoughts that only serve to bog us down.

On the emotional barometer, the tangy aroma of lemon aligns with, refreshes, and reinvigorates the mental body and shifts confusion and frustration to the inspired ease that flows with clear rational thought. Lemon stimulates the hippocampus to restore balance—the hippocampus is part of the limbic system, part of our back brain, that which is primal, reptilian. Apart from survival, the limbic system deals with fear, rage, and pleasure, and sets up memory patterns. How we deal with issues, store issues, and react to pain (physical or emotional) is unique to each of us. We can have similar experiences but we each react uniquely and in our own way, and unless we are prepared to expose our vulnerability and deal with it, then we cannot reach out and touch another. Exposing vulnerability need not feel threatening: exposure to one's self, preparedness to look at it, is all that is required—and remember confronting vulnerabilities can be done as slowly as we wish; baby steps still get us there.

When we feel our potential limited by overwhelming confusion and frustration, the shift to clarity and calm deliberation is a gift that unlocks awareness, and enhances our capacity for understanding. Our thoughts create how we feel. Our feelings create how we act. What if we really can change our mind and change our life?

Flower Essences

The highest resonance is between black tourmaline and Willow Bach Flower and Kapok Bush Australian Bush Flower Essences.

Willow is one of the Bach Flower Essence remedies for despondency or despair. Willow is useful for those times of resentment or upset at the unfairness of it all. Some of us can have a tendency to such despair, but it's possible for any of us to wrap ourselves snugly in the victim shawl and go to ground with thoughts and feelings of *Poor me...why me? Why did this have to happen? Why is this happening to me?* Sometimes we do not feel bitterness or anger, just that instantly recognizable flat feeling that swamps us for no specific reason and leads us down a foggy path into the overwhelming haze of the victim. We withdraw, we feel irritable, and we cannot be pleased, because no one understands, anyway.

Willow can facilitate transformation that restores mental/emotional balance and facilitates a shift from being one of life's victims to reveling in the feeling of being master of one's own fate. We willingly accept self-responsibility. We understand that we always play a part, and we are always gifted choice. We can choose to see every situation as we wish, and transformation brings an appreciation of the wellness and well-being that can flow from a change in perspective, and a willingness to jump in and live with the optimism and faith that comes from knowing that all is well and there is more than enough "good stuff" for all of us. There's a smorgasbord of good stuff to choose from and we embrace our innate knowingness and start tasting that which tempts us and happily leave the rest.

Kapok Bush is the Australian Bush Flower Essence remedy for apathy and resignation—those times when we are easily discouraged and feel resigned to the worse, or for those who have a tendency to give up easily, throw in the towel when the going gets tough. Life can be stressful; pain and illness can be stressful; relationships can be stressful; and sometimes it can all just feel too hard. We go through life halfhearted. Sure, we're okay; we're surviving; everything's okay, not too bad. But somewhere deep inside, there's a part of us that wants to scream, *You know what... it's not okay...feeling "okay" is not okay!*

The positive outcome is one of persistence, tenacity, preparedness, and willingness to "have a go." We choose to take responsibility for how we respond to the inevitable challenges along the way. We decide to respond rather than simply react with resignation because it all seems too hard. We see the inherent opportunity in every moment, clearly and rationally think it through, discern and discriminate that which serves our highest good, and when we choose to go for it, jump in and see it through to the best of our ability. We need only do our best, and on some days our best may be only ten per cent of what our best will be tomorrow—but today we need only do the best we can. I am reminded of a dear young boy who, at the age of seven, told me, *Never give up and never give in!* Bless him, he was living the transformation.

Archangels

The highest resonance is between black tourmaline and Archangel Raziel.

Archangel Raziel brings the wizard-like energy of the Divine that helps us see that life truly can be magical and that we have all the resources that we need, and infinite choice, in any and every moment.

Those who enjoy exploring esoteric concepts will find sage guidance for understanding Spirit, quantum physics, and sacred geometry; he also helps us understand the power of symbolism, psychic insight, and high magic, and helps us interpret dreams and vague memory snippets of past lives.

He protects those who call on him, and we feel safe as we explore the unknown; Raziel has greatly broadened my understanding of energetic alchemy, energetic shielding, clearing psychic attack, and Divine magic. His energy helps us work through perceived problems to resolution and is helpful for healing emotional pain.

Raziel stimulates curiosity and encourages a sense of adventure to explore that which is greater than us; he facilitates shifts in perception and healing on all levels, finding our life purpose, and brings a heightened awareness of All That Is. Innate intuition and awareness are amplified as we open up to Divine guidance. Manifestation pathways open up to us, seemingly out of nowhere, and success flows easily in ways we had never previously imagined as we play in the infinite field of possibilities and potentialities available to us.

. . . .

I have come to appreciate that energetic shifts can happen in a moment; shifts can be subtle and happen slowly over time; shifts can blindside us; and shifts can be welcomed with the open arms of awareness and gratitude—but they are ongoing in all of their wonderful guises. The synergy of this crystal combination has brought me such awareness.

Indeed, we are such masterful creators and create endless, and often colorful, opportunities for change and growth along the way, but I am now mindful that we always get to choose *if* we wish to play and then *how* we wish to play. There are infinite possibilities and our choices determine the growth.

The support of the black tourmaline synergistic combination has supported even my deepest look within the shadows, and my willingness to explore has brought an equally deep appreciation of the magic of manifestation and the wonder of life. I know the vibrational wellness and well-being that spring from acceptance of what is and a preparedness to live in wonder of All That Is. We embrace an appreciation and understanding that we are ever becoming—and sometimes we glimpse something intangible and wondrous, and contemplate *what if we are simply energy being human?*

Meditation Practices

By choosing to quiet the mind and use the black tourmaline synergistic combination, we unlock our door of awareness and open to the inherent magic in life—a life that we continually create. We embrace a sense of adventure to engage with life that is buoyed by a feeling of relaxed optimism. Doors open where once there were none and life shifts from tragical to truly magical, supported by awareness of the infinite field of possibilities and potentialities that is constant and there for each of us. We can choose to allow our Divinity to live through our humanity...and our choices. There is an elusive richness to a life that is regularly refreshed by quiet time alone in contemplation.

For the following meditations, please have at hand your crystal, essential oil, and crystal and flower essences. The crystal essence and combined flower essences may be taken in a single blend, or used separately, as is most convenient to you. The essential oil may certainly be vaporized in an oil burner to fill the meditation space, but as this is not always doable or convenient in some locations, please be assured that a few drops of essential oil on a tissue or handkerchief will serve you well at any time and in any setting—whether meditating at home or in the open air, or simply connecting in while waiting in line at the supermarket.

Sit in whatever way is comfortable for you—if seated in a chair, have your feet flat on the floor with no shoes. Ensure your back is straight by gently lifting your heart center. Relax your shoulders. Lengthen the back of the neck by slightly tilting the chin downward.

Take a couple of breaths and bring yourself to a place of quiet appreciation of this time that you are gifting you.

Meditation to Connect with the Black Tourmaline Synergy

This is often regarded as the simplest and "earthiest" of the three meditations using powerful black tourmaline in combination. In this meditation, we connect to the high vibrational energy that is created by the specific combination of these gifts from Mother Earth: black tourmaline stone, lemon essential oil, and a blend of black tourmaline, Willow, and Kapok Bush essences. As always, it is all about the synergy of the combination. I use this meditation whenever I feel in need of the stability, clarity, and expansive understanding that inevitably follow as I am empowered and uplifted. To connect with the black tourmaline synergy, you will need:

Black tourmaline crystal

Lemon essential oil

Willow and Kapok Bush flower essences

Black tourmaline crystal essence

- Place four drops of the combined Willow and Kapok Bush flower essences and black tourmaline crystal essence under your tongue. Take a breath.

- Anoint the black tourmaline with a drop of lemon essential oil. Inhale the uplifting, stimulating and cleansing fragrance as you gently rub the oil into the stone, breathing slowly and deeply. Take a breath.

- Cup the black tourmaline lightly in your hands—the fingertips of the right hand gently touch to the base of the left palm—and rest your hands comfortably in your lap. Take a breath and softly close your eyes.

- Feel the energy of the black tourmaline as it fills your cupped hands—for example, it may feel tingling, effervescent, light, heavy, or like your hands are suctioned together or they may expand apart during the session—there is no right way it should feel, and how it feels is right for you.

- Feel or imagine the energy moving up through your arms, through to the heart center, and radiating out to fill your entire being in whatever way feels right for you.

- Trust that the synergy of the combination will open up, ease, balance, heal, inspire, or enhance that which needs attention at this time.

- You may see color behind the closed eyes—maybe glittering flashes, maybe a kaleidoscope of various colors, or color that fades in and out, as the energy of the black tourmaline combination connects with various energy centers and your masterful Inner Being.

- Feel gratitude for any creative sparks, inspiration, feelings of acceptance and knowing, or awareness that come to you and let them go, trusting that all will be there for you when you come out of the meditation.

- Feel the energy. Be in wonder of the synergy of these combined gifts from Mother Earth. Luxuriate in the connection that is ever present and is you; allow it to fill you and expand you, and remain within that expansive grounded space for as long as you wish.

Meditation on the Essence of the Black Tourmaline Combination (with Affirmations)

Black tourmaline in combination grounds, inspires, and strengthens me, and this meditation is the most powerful for supporting change. Heartfelt decisions and intentions to release limitation and embrace creativity are transformational. Again, it is all about the combination's synergy that lifts the vibration of our physical, emotional, mental, and spiritual bodies, and the specific affirmations are an integral component of the synergy of this meditation practice. The affirmations allow and facilitate change in ways that continually surprise and delight me—the words remain unchanged each time, but the results are as different as I am each time I change and grow, and then return to this inspired black tourmaline affirmation practice.

- Please sit in your comfortable meditation position.

- Place four drops of your combined Willow and Kapok Bush flower essences and black tourmaline crystal essence under the tongue, anoint your black tourmaline with a drop of lemon essential oil and inhale a few drops of lemon from a tissue or handkerchief while holding your stone in lightly cupped hands.

- Settle into the position, close your eyes, and take a long, slow, deep breath, releasing any tension on the exhale. Repeat with two more breaths.

- Take your awareness behind the eyebrow center. This is the third eye chakra. The color is deep indigo or purple. See yourself sitting in the middle of this space—the one in the middle who intuitively knows.

- Breathe.

- Take your awareness to the crown above you. See it layered with the petals of a closed lotus flower and imagine those petals unfolding, opening to pure positive energy and the infinite field of possibilities.

- Allow the pure white light to illuminate and enliven the deep indigo purple of this space. Feel the energy flood in and cascade through the physical body.

- Breathe.

- Repeat this statement to yourself. *I am a master creator.*

- Breathe.

- Take your awareness to just below the navel center. This is the sacral chakra. The color is a rich orange. See the pelvic area as a golden bowl filled with vibrant orange liquid. You sit in the middle on a giant lotus leaf, perfectly balanced, fully supported.

- Breathe.

- No matter which way you choose to move, the liquid always returns to balance with you perfectly supported in the middle.

- Breathe.

- Repeat this statement to yourself. *I am gifted infinite possibilities.*

- Breathe.

- Take your awareness to the chest center. This is the heart chakra—the middle chakra, that which bridges the upper three and lower three. The color is vibrant emerald or forest green. See yourself in the middle on a vibrant pink and white lotus flower atop a green lotus leaf. You are seated in your heart, the center of unconditional love.

- Breathe.

- See the heart center flooded with Divine energy from above as life-force energy rises to meet it from below. You are supported in Love from above and below.

- Repeat this statement to yourself. *My Divinity lives through my humanity. I am energy being human.*

- Breathe.

- This powerful energy from your heart center floods down your arms and out through your hands to touch the world. You are fully supported and in your power as you choose to act from your heart.

- Repeat the full affirmation, feeling Spirit, or your innate Divinity, Higher Self, or beautiful Inner Being speaking to you. *You are a master creator, open to the infinite field of possibilities and potentialities. Your Divinity lives through your humanity. You are energy being human.*

- Breathe. Remain in this space, feeling this space, for as long as it feels comfortable, or as long as your schedule allows.

- When you are ready, take a deep breath and bring your awareness back to the crown. See the petals of the lotus flower closing once again—yours to open at will, and close at will.

- Take another long, slow breath.

- Bring your awareness back into the body. Wiggle your toes and fingers, gently move your hands and your head, and open your eyes to bring your awareness fully back into this moment.

- Express gratitude for All That Is and the gift of grace ... and be aware that your Source is even more grateful for all that you are, and all that you are becoming. And so It is.

Meditation to Connect with Archangel Raziel, Higher Self, and Spirit Guides and Teachers

This simple meditation is often favored by those who already enjoy working with archangels, Spirit, guides, or teachers, but please remember that they are all aspects of our innate Divinity or essence. Whether you wish to connect with the energy of Archangel Raziel for support to explore the wonder of choices and potentialities available to you, or whether you wish to connect to your own Inner Being, the synergy of the black tourmaline combination will powerfully support your heartfelt intention to be present in the moment and to be open to allow that which is there for you to flow to you.

- Please sit in your comfortable meditation position.

- If you have a question or a situation with which you would like clarity or guiding support, bring that to mind.

- If you have a favorite invocation or preferred ritual for connecting to your teachers, guides or Spirit, please use that which feels right for you.

- Place four drops of your combined Willow and Kapok Bush flower essences and black tourmaline crystal essence under the tongue, anoint your black tourmaline with a drop of lemon essential oil, inhale a few drops of the cleansing stimulating lemon oil from a tissue or handkerchief and throughout the meditation if you feel inspired to do so, and hold your stone in lightly cupped hands.

- Settle into the position, close your eyes, and take a long, slow, deep breath, releasing any tension on the exhale. Repeat with two more breaths.

- Feeling relaxed, still, and present to the moment, please state your intentions. *I am present for all that is here for me. I am listening, and you are welcome.*

- Breathe and release any tension with a long exhalation.

- The soft sound of the breath mirrors the tranquil space of silence where inner peace, tranquility, and harmony are found. Feel the breath, hear the breath, and allow for any awareness of connection that follows.

- Feel deep appreciation and gratitude for this time of connection to a Divine messenger, teacher, or aspect of Oneness, and come out of the meditation whenever you are ready.

Please know that no matter what you feel or do not feel during the meditation, any question you have asked has been answered, any clarity you are seeking has been forthcoming, and any connection you desired has been facilitated by the synergy of the high vibrational combination of black tourmaline crystal, lemon essential oil, and the black tourmaline, Willow, and Kapok Bush essence blend, and Archangel Raziel. Your conscious awareness and sense of creativity in every moment, understanding of the infinite possibilities available to you and the infinite potentialities for you to be however you wish to be, and the wonder of choosing to allow your innate Divinity to live through your choices have been awakened and heightened. If this is not a familiar practice for you, please be reassured that enhanced connection is always facilitated and clarity and answers always provided. Sometimes guidance will flow into your consciousness during the practice, sometimes you will be inspired to pick up a particular book, or turn onto a certain radio or television channel, or bump into someone as you go about your day. The answers and clarity always flow, but we do not always get to micromanage how they come to us. Indeed, trusting in our inherent guidance will always deliver that which we seek in the quickest, most direct, and life-enhancing way ... we just need to trust.

Remember, it is in the smallest of moments that miracles happen and the magic of Raziel and associated teachers and guides, including your Higher Self, facilitated through the synergy of the black tourmaline combination is indeed inspired.

Conclusion

I am so grateful for the store of knowledge and information that has been documented and stored across time and which has facilitated my continual growth and supported my passion for wholeness, wellness, and well-being. The information shared in this book is intended to add to the store of information and knowledge, and not intended to dismiss or replace traditional practices and information that have come before.

I have developed the crystal combinations through immersing myself in the process and surrendering to the potentialities that have opened up for me, and I have learned that the synergistic combinations and practices consistently enhance the vibrational frequency of each crystal and therefore facilitate and enrich our connections to Higher Self, Spirit, and All That Is. It is in that space of heightened vibration and connection to the energy of Oneness that we each return to our innate vibrational balance, wellness, and well-being. It feels very joyful and very grounded, light yet earthy; it is a sense of wellness and well-being that I find very balanced, real, and tangible as I go about my day.

When our chosen daily routine includes the synergistic combinations and practices that bring together these gifts from Mother Earth and Beyond, we step out feeling connected, nurtured, sustained, and safe, wrapped in an aura of sensual comfort with the solidarity of our rock resonating its protection. I am excited at the possibilities and potentialities that may open for you as you explore that which is on offer. I am grateful for the opportunity to share with you that which continues to serve me well, and honored that you have chosen to share some time exploring *Crystal Resonance*.

I am always thrilled to hear from readers and to answer any questions that you might have, so please feel free to contact me for any information through my website, **www.kerrynelsonselman.com.au.**

Reference Tables

CRYSTAL SYNERGISTIC COMBINATIONS REFERENCE TABLE Crystals, Essential Oils, Flower Essences, and Archangels				
Crystals	Essential Oils	Bach Flower Essences	Australian Bush Flower Essences	Archangels
Amethyst	Lavender	Cerato	Bluebell	Zadkiel
Aquamarine	Lemongrass	Star of Bethlehem	Slender Rice Flower	Jophiel
Aventurine, Green	Bergamot	Crab Apple	Philotheca	Chamuel
Carnelian	Ylang-Ylang	Scleranthus	Southern Cross	Uriel
Citrine	Sandalwood	Wild Oat	Tall Yellow Top	Jeremiel
Fluorite	Neroli	Agrimony	Macrocarpa	Raphael
Jasper, Red	Jasmine	Gentian	Sturt Desert Rose	Raguel

CRYSTAL SYNERGISTIC COMBINATIONS REFERENCE TABLE (CTD.)				
Crystals, Essential Oils, Flower Essences, and Archangels				
Crystals	Essential Oils	Bach Flower Essences	Australian Bush Flower Essences	Archangels
Moonstone	Carrot Seed	Impatiens	Fringed Violet	Metatron
Quartz, Clear	Frankincense and Neroli	Centaury	Green Spider Orchid	Michael
Quartz, Rose	Frankincense	Holly	Bush Fuchsia	Haniel
Selenite	Neroli	Elm	Bush Iris	Gabriel
Tiger Iron	Frankincense	Walnut	Red Grevillea	Haniel
Tourmaline, Black	Lemon	Willow	Kapok Bush	Raziel

Archangels represent specific aspects of Divinity that resonate synergistically with the above combinations from the Earth. However, awareness of resonance or connection with the archangel in a particular synergistic combination is always a matter of choice...and, as always, the choice remains with us. Please remember, there are no right or wrong combinations when working with the gifts from the Earth and Beyond, but some gifts combine synergistically to produce a combination that can vibrationally lift us to a place of Oneness that facilitates vibrational wellness and well-being.

ARCHANGELS REFERENCE TABLE Crystal Synergistic Combinations Listed by Archangels				
Archangels	Crystals	Essential Oils	Bach Flower Essences	Australian Bush Flower Essences
Chamuel	Green Aventurine	Bergamot	Crab Apple	Philotheca
Gabriel	Selenite	Neroli	Elm	Bush Iris
Haniel	Rose Quartz	Frankincense	Holly	Bush Fuchsia
Haniel	Tiger Iron	Frankincense	Walnut	Red Grevillea
Jeremiel	Citrine	Sandalwood	Wild Oat	Tall Yellow Top
Jophiel	Aquamarine	Lemongrass	Star of Bethlehem	Slender Rice Flower
Metatron	Moonstone	Carrot Seed	Impatiens	Fringed Violet
Michael	Clear Quartz	Frankincense and Neroli	Centaury	Green Spider Orchid
Raguel	Red Jasper	Jasmine	Gentian	Sturt Desert Rose
Raphael	Fluorite	Neroli	Agrimony	Macrocarpa
Raziel	Black Tourmaline	Lemon	Willow	Kapok Bush
Uriel	Carnelian	Ylang-ylang	Scleranthus	Southern Cross
Zadkiel	Amethyst	Lavender	Cerato	Bluebell

Meditation Affirmations

I am gifted wisdom and understanding. I am gifted trust.
I am gifted connection ... there is no separation and
I am forgiven. I am energy being human. (Amethyst)

I speak my truth. I am gifted grace and harmony when I speak my truth.
I am my own true north. I am energy being human. (Aquamarine)

I can see clearly now. I am powerfully protected.
I am safe to choose from the heart. I am energy
being human. (Green Aventurine)

I cannot fail. I am gifted innate perfection and balance.
I can be however I choose to be and shine brightly.
I am energy being human. (Carnelian)

I am revitalized and uplifted. I am gifted abundance and prosperity.
I am of infinite value. I am energy being human. (Citrine)

I am refreshed and renewed, aligned and in tune. I am gifted infinite
choices. I am fully supported. I am energy being human. (Fluorite)

All is clear and simple. I am gifted ease and flow. I am in integrity when
I choose and act from the heart. I am energy being human. (Red Jasper)

I feel equally calm and excited about what is to come.
I find calm and balance in any storm. My power comes from a
soft gentle center. I am energy being human. (Moonstone)

I can be however I choose to be. I can be fearless in my choices.
I can be all that I choose to be. I am energy being human. (Clear Quartz)

I am loving and peaceful. I am fully supported as I adapt to
change. I am gifted unconditional love and have infinite
worth. I am energy being human. (Rose Quartz)

I expect a miracle. I am ordinary, but I can choose to
live an extraordinary life. I shine my Divinity through my
humanity. I am energy being human. (Selenite)

Goddess/God lives within me, as me. I am perfectly poised in the dance of the
Divine Feminine and Masculine. I am nurtured, sustained, and protected by
the heart of the peaceful warrior. I am energy being human. (Tiger Iron)

I am a master creator. I am gifted infinite possibilities. My Divinity lives
through my humanity. I am energy being human. (Black Tourmaline)

Glossary of Terms

Archangels—Divine messengers and spiritual guides with specialized focus representing aspects of Divinity; they are light beings, pure vibration.

Astral body—alternate name for Emotional body—see Emotional body.

Aura—another name for Biomagnetic field and Etheric body—see Etheric body.

Avatar—one who lives and is enlightened; avatars are often great philosophers, spiritual teachers, and miracle workers.

Biomagnetic field—another name for Aura and Etheric body—see Etheric body.

Causal body—alternate name for Spiritual body—see Spiritual body.

Chakra—energy center—many are scattered throughout body, but the seven prime chakras from the base of the torso up are: base or root chakra (Mooladhara); sacral chakra (Swadhisthana); solar plexus chakra (Manipura); heart chakra (Anahata); throat chakra (Vishuddhi); third eye chakra (Ajna); and crown chakra (Sahasrara).

Emotional body—the invisible biomagnetic energy layer that surrounds all living beings and sits between the Etheric and Mental bodies—it is the layer closer to the body physical than the Mental body, another reminder of the powerful impact on the body physical of how we feel in any given moment, and the life-enhancing practice of taking responsibility for how we feel.

Etheric body—another term for the subtle Aura or Biomagnetic field that is the inner invisible energy layer that sheathes the body physical.

Lightworker—one who lives with a deep commitment to work for the highest good to facilitate enhanced spiritual energy in and on the Earth.

Mental body—the invisible biomagnetic energy layer that surrounds all living beings and sits between the Spiritual and the Emotional bodies, relating to the mental aspects of being.

Merkaba—(also Merkabah) in Judaic text the Merkaba is the chariot of God—it is a vehicle of light constructed and powered by the Angels under the charge of Archangel Metatron. Today, this configuration contained within the circle, All That Is, embodies sacred geometry. It is a spirit body that facilitates connection with Spirit and the infinite field outside of time, space and dimension, and is configured into a holographic shape known as Metatron's Cube or the Flower of Life representing that which is the basis of all there is and contains all there is.

Sacred geometry—traditionally the sacred symbolism attached to shapes, numbers, and patterns, and embodied in buildings of worship and art across time. Today this art-science is seen as representing the harmony of the dance of the universe hidden in symbolic shapes and number patterns and holding the key to the universal code of all that ever was, is, and ever will be; for Plato, a metaphor for the universal order. It embraces concepts such as fractals, resonance, vibration, the sacred spiritual spiral, the Fibonacci Cascade and the inherent harmony of Phi, the number behind the golden ratio or golden section, and that which is Divine proportion and appears throughout nature. For example, the circle is the most revered: it is the line without beginning and without end; it is infinite; it is complete, all there is; it is the Mother-Father God. Its center is equidistant from the outside circumference, thus the center contains all there is, the center of creation, infinite and all powerful. If we consider words as symbols for thoughts and ideas, then numbers can be seen as symbols of the Divine, Divine order and of the infinite Universe—all that ever has been, is, and ever will be. Ancient Greek and Egyptian avatars and scholars described geometry as frozen music—in other words, a moment of harmony frozen in time and outside of time and space. There is sacred geometry in the rhythm and meter of many texts, particularly those that sing with Spirit.

Soul—many interchange the terms Soul and Spirit but, for me, the Soul or Soul body is that which contains memory or the sum total of all that we have experienced since separation—it is that part of our Spirit that contains the sum total of all we have been across time and space.

Spiritual body—the invisible biomagnetic energy layer that surrounds all living beings, providing the skin, as it were, between the subtle bodies and All That Is—much as the skin of the body physical protects and supports us, so too our spiritual body protects and supports us while expanding out to add all that we choose to be to the mass consciousness, and so supporting Universal growth.

Spirit—for me, our Spirit is outside of time and space, timeless if you will; it is that part of us that is connected to All That Is, that which is a spark of the Universal Spirit, or Universal Mind; it is the spark of Divinity within each of us.

Subtle bodies—the layers or energy fields that surround the body physical of all living beings, much like one would view a hologram: Physical body, Etheric body, Emotional body, Mental body, and Spiritual body.

Bibliography

Bach, E. *Heal Thyself: An Explanation of the Real Cause and Cure of Disease.* Saffron Walden, Essex: The C.W. Daniel Company, 1931.

Chancellor, P.M. *Illustrated Handbook of the Bach Flower Remedies: An Authoritative Guide to Natural Healing with Flower Essences.* London: Vermilion, 2005.

Davis, P. *Subtle Aromatherapy.* London: Random House, 2011.

Gurudas. *Gem Elixirs and Vibrational Healing, Vol. I.* Boulder, CO: Cassandra Press, 1985.

Gurudas. *Gem Elixirs and Vibrational Healing, Vol. II.* Boulder, CO: Cassandra Press, 1986.

Gurudas. *Flower Essences and Vibrational Healing.* Boulder CO: Cassandra Press, 1986.

Hall, J. *The Crystal Bible: The Definitive Guide to Crystals and Their Uses.* London: Hachette, 2009.

Scheffer, M. *Bach Flower Therapy: Theory and Practice*. Rochester, VT: Healing Arts Press, 1988.

Schiller, C. and Schiller, D. *The Aromatherapy Encyclopedia: A Concise Guide to Over 395 Plant Oils*, 2nd ed. Laguna Beach, CA: Basic Health Publications, 2012.

Vallak, J. *Angelology: A Guide to the Angelic, Devic and Nature Spirit Realms*. Leongatha, Vic.: Junitta Vallak, 2009.

Virtue, D. *Archangels and Ascended Masters: A Guide to Working and Healing with Divinities and Deities*. London: Hay House, 2003.

Virtue, D. *Archangels 101: How to Connect Closely with Archangels Michael, Raphael, Gabriel, Uriel, and Others for Healing, Protection, and Guidance*. Carlsbad, CA: Hay House, 2010.

White, I. *Australian Bush Flower Essences*. Sydney: Bantam, 1991.

Zeck, R. *Blossoming Heart: Aromatherapy for Healing and Transformation*. East Ivanhoe, Vic.: Aroma Tours, 2003.

About the Author

Kerry lives on the rugged and inspiring far south coast of New South Wales in Australia. She holds advanced diplomas in Naturopathy, Herbal Medicine, and Nutritional Medicine, Master Aromatherapist Diploma, Diploma in Advanced Crystal Healing, and certificates in various forms of Reiki. She is a professional practitioner of naturopathy, herbal medicine, clinical and holistic aromatherapy, nutritional medicine, crystal healing, Vibrational Oneness, traditional Usui Reiki, Newlife Reiki Seichim, life coaching, and holistic counseling linking body, mind, and spirit.

Although her choice is natural medicine, Kerry understands that, whether we choose natural or orthodox medicine, the vital component of all wellness and well-being is the healing and rebalancing that must take place mentally and emotionally—and it is this knowing that stimulates her enthusiasm for energetic practices as part of any holistic treatment program. Kerry is the passionate creator and Teacher Practitioner of Vibrational Oneness™ practice and an equally passionate Reiki Master/Teacher, and is also available for workshops on crystals, essential oils, flower essences, mindfulness and guided meditation. She brings together all of her knowledge and passions in her writing.

Kerry knows how it feels to choose to walk a different path. After half a lifetime in Sydney, satisfying their desire for a tree-change away from the city allowed Kerry and her husband, Gary, the opportunity to change their minds and change their lives. They took a decision to opt for a simpler life … and so their journey forked onto a new path. Today, life holds little similarity to that which has long passed.

Her love of gardening resurfaced and with it a love of growing and using her own herbs; Kerry's deep respect for the abundance that can come from the Earth is in the genes—she can trace her heritage back through a long line of home-herbalists, nurserymen, and orchardists. A subsequent move down to the wild beauty of the far south coast brought with it new opportunities and *Wellness by the Sea* was launched. Kerry now shares her passion for the wonder of life and the forgiving nature of the body through her writing, and through her practice as a natural therapist. Daring to change can be challenging, but can bring great joy.

Whether writing books of self-empowerment or manuals to accompany her workshops, Kerry generously shares her knowledge and passions with the intention to inspire, uplift, enhance a sense of wellness and well-being, and to simply be enjoyed. She comes to her writing and her healing with a sense of passion, ease, acceptance, and knowing that the highest good is always served by her intention to connect with that special place within each of us that facilitates wellness and well-being.

Awareness of the choices we make in our daily lives will always facilitate a path to feeling better, whether physically, emotionally, mentally, or spiritually; we take responsibility for our own health and happiness, and free all others of the burden of providing it for us. The choices we make will always shine from us, be reflected in the world around us, and add to the delicious texture of Life.

Index